John E. Taylor

**Half-Hours at the Sea-Side**

Or, Recreations with marine objects

John E. Taylor

**Half-Hours at the Sea-Side**
*Or, Recreations with marine objects*

ISBN/EAN: 9783337418397

Printed in Europe, USA, Canada, Australia, Japan

Cover: Foto ©Andreas Hilbeck / pixelio.de

More available books at **www.hansebooks.com**

# HALF HOURS AT THE SEA-SIDE;

OR,

## RECREATIONS WITH MARINE OBJECTS.

BY

### J. E. TAYLOR, F.G.S.,

AUTHOR OF "GEOLOGY OF MANCHESTER AND NEIGHBOURHOOD," "GEOLOGICAL STORIES,"
ETC.

LONDON:
ROBERT HARDWICKE, 192, PICCADILLY.
1872.

LONDON:
PRINTED BY WILLIAM CLOWES AND SONS, STAMFORD STREET
AND CHARING CROSS.

# PREFACE.

THE object in compiling the following pages has been to render the sea-side visit (now almost an annual occurrence to most people) more interesting and instructive. Nearly all the creatures described are obtainable by the student at our principal watering-places. An attempt has been made to introduce the subject-matter in as methodical and scientific a manner as possible, so that each chapter might be a sketch of the natural history, classification, and affinities of the animals mentioned. In this manner, the young beginner will be brought into direct acquaintance with the first principles of zoology. Where possible, the embryological relations of the various forms, and the geological antiquity of the genus or family to which they belong, have been introduced. Thus it will be seen that, apart from the interest attached to the study and observation of the habits and economy of our commonest sea-side objects, there are also connected with them some of the profoundest speculations of modern philosophy.

*July 1st,* 1872.

# CONTENTS.

## I.

### HALF AN·HOUR WITH THE WAVES.

The pleasures of the sea-side.—Antiquity of the ocean.—Space formerly occupied by the gases composing water.—Forces locked up in our seas.—Relation of atmosphere to ditto.—Theories of the tides.—Peculiarity of sea-air, how caused.—Waste of our coast-line.—How waves are formed.—Currents of the ocean.—Their beneficial action on marine life.—Depths of the sea.—Saltness of ditto.—Evidences of wave-action in ancient deposits.—Relation of marine objects to dissolved minerals, &c.—How the latter are disposed of . . . . . . . . . . Pages 1 to 18

## II.

### HALF AN HOUR WITH PREPARATIONS.

Equipment of the zoological student.—Fewness of objects required.—Advantage of the microscope.—Wet days at the sea-side.—Bell-glasses for temporary aquaria.—Anemone-collecting.—Local guide books.—Implements, &c., required for shore-zoologising.—How to set about the latter.—The mysteries of a rock-pool.—*Pholades.*—The tow-net, how made.—The study of deeper sea-life.—The trawlmen and their " rubbish."—Out trawling.—Description of the trawl, &c. . . . . . . . . . . . . . . Pages 19 to 33

## III.

### HALF AN HOUR WITH SEA-WEEDS.

How to collect sea-weeds.—Abundance of species between tides.—The three groups of sea-weeds.—*Melanosperms*, their larger size.—Roots of sea-weeds.—The "Bladder-wrack."—Its air bladders.—Fructification of sea-weeds.—The Serrated Wrack.—The Knotted Wrack.—The Small Wrack.—Laminaria.—Halidrys.—The *Rhodosperms*.—Their deeper-water habit.—Beauty of many species.—*Polysiphonia.—Chlylocladia.—Corallina officinalis.*—Capability of this and other species to secrete lime.—*Delesseria.—Ptilota, Griffithsia, Rhodymenia, Porphyra, Plocamium,* &c.—The "Peacock" Laver.—"Carrageen," or Irish Moss.—The *Chlorosperms.—Enteromorpha, Ulva, Cladophora, Bryopsis,* &c.—How to mount sea-weeds.—Necessity of marine vegetation to marine life, &c. . . . . . . . . . . Pages 34 to 50

## IV.

### HALF AN HOUR WITH SPONGES.

Popular notion of a sponge.—British sponges.—*Chalina oculata.*—Its general structure.—The three divisions of sponges.—Ornamental character of silicated sponges.—The "Glass Rope."—Calcareous sponges.—Their geological antiquity.—*Ventriculites,* &c.—Keratose sponges.—Structure of *Grantia.—Halina, Leuconia, Microciona, Pachymatisma,* &c.—The boring sponges.—Their geological antiquity.—*Halichondria* species.—General structure described.—Economic value of sponges.—Their great importance in geological operations.—Their instrumentality in forming flints, &c. . . . . . . . . . . . . Pages 51 to 69

## V.

### HALF AN HOUR WITH SEA-WORMS.

The study of natural history.—False popular notions respecting "imperfect" animals.—The earth-worm and sea-worm.

—The two great groups of sea-worms, *Tubicola* and *Errantia.*
—*Serpula,* their abundance and general structure.—Geological antiquity of the group.—*Spirorbis.*—The Crystal Palace aquarium.—*Sabella, Terebella,* &c.—The *Errantia.*—The "Lob-worms."—Antiquity of the family.—Physiological structure.—The "Sea-centipede."—Alternation of generations.—*Eunice, Polynoe, Phyllodoce, Nemertes,* &c.—The *Sipunculus.*—Harmony of creation . . . Pages 69 to 83

VI.

HALF AN HOUR WITH CORALLINES.

General notions respecting these objects.—Their structure.—Relations to the *Hydras.*—Tubularians, or "Pipe-corallines."—The various species described.—The Sertularians, or "sea-firs."—Their general structure.—The five genera.—The "Bottle-brush" coralline, "Sickle" coralline, "Sea-hair" coralline, "Sea-oak" coralline, "Fern" coralline, "Squirrel's-tail" coralline, "Sea-cypress" coralline, &c.—The *Campanularidæ.*—Their reproduction in medusoids, or jelly-fish.—The "Bird's-head" coralline, "Lobster's-horn" coralline, &c.—Alternation of generation in the group.—Relation of the jelly-fish to them, &c. Pages 84 to 104

VII.

HALF AN HOUR WITH JELLY-FISH.

The appearance of jelly-fish when stranded, and when in the sea.—Natural history of the group.—Zoological division of ditto.—The "Crimson-ringed" jelly-fish.—Its general structure.—Stages through which the young pass before reaching adult.—*Hydra tuba,* &c.—*Cyanea, Thaumantia, Turris, Sarsia, Æquora.*—The "Portuguese Man-of-war."—*Velella.*—The Beröe.—Its beauty.—Lucernaria.—Small quantity of solid matter in jelly-fish.—Production of marine phosphorescence, &c. . . . . . . . . . Pages 105 to 117

## VIII.

#### HALF AN HOUR WITH SEA-ANEMONES.

Popularity of the study of anemones.—Favourites in the marine aquarium.—No. of British species.—Their zoological characters and divisions.—General structure.—Comparison with corallines. — *Actinoloba*.— *Sagartia*. — Nettling power and organs of latter described.—Mimicry.—" Daisy anemone," " Cave " ditto, " Rosy " ditto.—Mr. Gosse's description of latter.—" Orange-disked " anemone, " Parasitic " anemone, &c.—*Adamsia*.—The " Opelet," " Beadlet," &c.—Longevity and hardy nature of latter.—The " Crass," " Strawberry " anemone, &c. . . . . . . . . . Pages 118 to 137

## IX.

#### HALF AN HOUR WITH SEA-MATS AND SQUIRTS.

The Greek physicists.—The sea as a life producer.—General character of sea-mats.—The *Flustra*.—Zoological relations of the group.—Its general structure illustrated.—Relations to the *Brachiopoda*.—The various species described.—The *Tunicata*, or " sea-squirts."—Their zoological characters.—The Ascidians.—Their structure.—Formation of cellulose in outer skin. — *Cynthia*, or " currant-squirter." — The *Botryllus*.—Species described.—*Clavelina, Lepralia*, &c.—The *Salpa*.—Its alternation of generations, &c. Pages 138 to 155

## X.

#### HALF AN HOUR WITH SEA-URCHINS AND STAR-FISH.

General structure of the above.—That of the Echinus detailed.—Physiological organisation.—Microscopical structure, &c.—*Pedicellaria*.—Spicules of different species.—The *Spatangus*, " Cushion-stars," &c.—The " five-fingered star-fish."—General structure of the class.—What they feed upon.—*Ophiura, Solaster*, &c. — The " Brittle stars."—Professor Forbes on ditto.—*Ophiocoma*.—Mr. Kitton's description of hooks, &c.—Different species of " Brittle stars " described.—The *Encrinites*. — Their geological antiquity. — The " Feather-stars."—The sea-cucumbers.—Spiculæ of ditto, &c. . . . . . . . . . . . Pages 156 to 179

## XI.

HALF AN HOUR WITH SHELL-FISH (UNIVALVES).

Beauty and popularity of shells.—Mathematical laws of construction.—Moseley on ditto.—Divisions of the group.—The *Cephalopoda*, or "Cuttle-fish."—Geological antiquity of many groups.—The "Octopus."—Physiological details of the structure of "Cuttle-fish."—Calamaries and squids.—Sepia.—"Sea-grapes," the eggs of Cuttle-fish.—Loligo.—The *Pteropoda*.—The *Gasteropoda* division of mollusca.—Naked-gilled ditto.—Univalves.—Limpet, Chitons, Trochus, Littorina, Nassa, Cyprea, Purpura, Natica, Dentalium.—Whelks, &c.—Egg-cases of latter, &c. . . Pages 179 to 204

## XII.

HALF AN HOUR WITH SHELL-FISH (BIVALVES).

Fertility of mollusca.—Geological importance of their valves. —The *Brachiopoda*.—Their geological antiquity.—Relation to sea-mats.—Their physiological structure.—The *Lamellibranchiata*.—General structure.—Mussels, "Razor-shells," Scallops, &c.—Mr. Gosse's description of latter.—*Pholas*: its boring powers.—Speculation on ditto.—How achieved. —The Mactras, Tellinas, Donax, &c.—*Mya arenaria* and *truncata*.—Thracia, Tapes, "Otter-shells," &c.—Astartes, Lucina, Cyprina, Crenella, Nucula, Leda, Pectunculus, Pinna, &c.—The smaller species . . . . Pages 205 to 227

## XIII.

HALF AN HOUR WITH CRUSTACEA.

Changes in the young of Crustacea.—Relation of barnacles to crabs and lobsters.—Balanus, Scalpellum, Lepas, &c.—Transformations of former.—The physiological structure of the Cirripedia.—Division of Crustacea into groups described.—Physiological characters detailed.—The "Spider-Crabs."—The great, or common crab.—Moulting of Crustacea.—Wood on ditto.—" Shore " crab," " Porcelain " crab, "Pea" crabs, "Nut" crabs, "Angled" crab, "Masked" crab, "Northern Stone" crab, "Spiny" crab, "Velvet Swimming" crab, &c.—Hermit crabs.—The *Pycnogonidæ*. —*Pallene, Nymphon,* &c.—Squat lobsters.—Spiny lobsters, *Gammarus.*—Prawns and Shrimps.—Parasites of ditto.— Amphipods, &c.—Conclusion . . . . . Pages 228 to 260

# HALF HOURS AT THE SEA-SIDE.

## I.

HALF AN HOUR WITH THE WAVES.

MANKIND has found something exhilarating in the "many-sounding sea" from the time when the Ten Thousand Greeks sent up their glad shout on seeing it, to this modern period, when we run down to Brighton for an eight hours' sniff. Its fresh salt smell is more fragrant than a bed of violets to the choked nostrils of town dwellers. There are few of us who will not be frank enough to own that some of the happiest days we can call to our remembrance were spent by the sea-side. Who has not felt the luxury of throwing himself on the yielding sands—which adjusted themselves to his form better than any bed of feathers—and given himself up to the simple childish pleasure of listening to the waves as they broke against the strand, and ran in shallow ripples to his feet! The enjoyment, when analysed, is about as simple as could be imagined, and yet do we know of any deeper or more enduring? Nowhere so much as at the sea-side do we enjoy the simple luxury of mere existence. The healthy bracing of the nerves, the vigorous appetite induced by the sea air, and the joyous spirits which rise in consequence, seem to endow us with a new life.

We think it possible just to indicate sufficient employment when thus engaged to render this enjoyment more complete. We would not crowd the time so as to "make it a toil of a pleasure," but simply use the incidents as so many pegs on which to hang richer and more enduring interest. There are few, even among the most careless and indolent, who, when laid at full length on the sands, have not amused themselves by some little occurrence, if it be only enjoying the frantic efforts of a crab to get on his legs, after the aforesaid visitor has turned him on his back. But " the eye brings with it the power of seeing," and thus one who is even slightly acquainted with the " common objects of the seashore " can enjoy incidents which the more careless would pass by.

Truly, even to a thoughtless mind, this great ocean is enough to set one a-thinking. We know that Byron's remarks on it are even more scientifically true than the poet thought—

"Times writes no wrinkle on thine azure brow,
Such as creation's dawn beheld, thou rollest now!"

Far back as the science of geology can go, with all its seemingly extravagant demand on the article of time, the earliest and oldest rocks were formed along sea-bottoms, just as sediments are forming at the present time. Living creatures then enjoyed the pleasure of their lowly existence. The great ocean was composed of *water*, as it is now—was agitated by tides, hurricanes, and storms. Its ripples broke against nameless and forgotten shores, as they are now spending themselves at our very feet. The whole animal and vegetable worlds have since then been progressing, until they have ascended from the animalcule to the man—from the diatom to the oak. But the sea has never changed its character. Like its Maker, it is " the same yesterday, to-day, and for ever." It has been the great menstruum of Life; and along its floors have been laid the foundations of continents, and the solid materials of mountain chains.

Whatever we may think of the doctrine of evolution, few will deny the broad evidences of design which appear in the combination of two gases to such a degree as to make up a volume of water like that which fills the oceans and seas, the lakes and rivers of the globe. What a space must have been taken up by this hydrogen and oxygen before they were combined and condensed into water! One can hardly wonder at the diffused and attenuated condition of that "world-stuff" which forms the nebulæ, and of which our own planet possibly consisted before God

"Fashioned it and hardened it
Into the great, bright, useful thing it is."

Quite as suggestive is the fact that ever since the water of the sea was formed it has possibly never been altered. It has acted as the great reservoir from which solar force has lifted just the quantity of moisture necessary to fertilise the dry land, and so to support terrestrial animal and vegetable life. The meteorological action of this moisture, whether as rain, rivers, currents of the sea, tides, &c., during countless myriads of ages, has worn down and dissolved many a pre-adamite continent, and strewn their *débris* along old sea-bottoms. There could, therefore, have been no solid dry land such as we have it, if there had been no seas. Certainly, if the formation and perpetuation of an agency so vast and important be not an act of design, we must confess we never considered anything which better deserved the name.

What latent force lies in this great aqueous reservoir! Professor Tyndall tells us there is more electricity enclosed in a single drop of water than is exhibited during an ordinary thunderstorm. What a fearfully latent power, therefore, must be locked up in the mighty volume of water which composes our oceans and seas! Enough, if liberated, instantly to reduce the solid globe to cosmical dust! Is it here that the force which held matter apart when the earth was part of an extended nebula has been condensed? If so, combined with the remainder, which even more potentially keeps the attenuated particles forming our atmosphere apart, one cannot but recognise the arrangement as wonderful. Certainly the force thus operating must have come from somewhere, and been confined, like the Genii of the "Arabian Nights," ever since life began on our planet, in its present aqueous and aërial slavery. Between these two elements of air and water we may recognise a wonderful relation. The denser ocean is influenced largely by the other ocean of air which wraps round the globe. The changes in the latter produced by heat and cold, which we name breezes, winds, gales, or hurricanes, according to their intensity, have the power of gently rippling the surface of the sea, or of raising it into mighty billows. In either case we can see how important these disturbing forces are to the life of the sea—how they mechanically mix atmospheric air with the water, and thus render it perpetually fit to support the marvellous abundance of organic forms which crowd the ocean, even to its minutest drop. Without the winds agitating the surface, the tides constantly mingling its waters, and its great currents traversing warm and cold regions like so many arteries, it would be literally impossible for marine life to exist. These mechanical agencies keep it fresh and pure; and the principle of circulation which prevails in the human body affords us no bad illustration of the plan by which the waters of the sea are kept in a state of eternal but beneficial commotion.

Of all these agencies at work, none is so powerful

as that of the tides. How strange it seems that our satellite, the moon, although placed nearly a quarter of a million of miles away from the earth, should nevertheless be able to exert an unseen influence upon the oceans and seas of the globe. The law of attraction silently exerts its force across that wide gulf, and thus the moon pulls or draws each part of the earth that happens to be turned immediately under her towards herself. The solid part of the globe she cannot affect—the component parts are already operated upon by forces too strong to admit of it. But wherever there is matter whose ultimate particles are so freely and loosely bound together as in water, there will the lunar influence be felt. Thus the moon's *pull* will result, out in the open sea, in one huge wave being drawn upwards, and this wave we call tidal. It travels onwards as the earth revolves on her axis, and, when it reaches continents or large islands, straits, channels, &c., it rushes up the narrow areas and often rises in height on account of being dammed up. Winds long prevailing may retard its progress, and thus produce a lower tide than usual; or they may assist the lunar influence, and thus effect a higher one. Currents may be and often are produced by tides meeting, after circling or skirting islands or mainlands, and "rough seas" be the consequence. These daily "tides" would occur exactly every twelve hours if the moon were absolutely stationary. But, seeing that she herself has a revolution to make, and that she has slowly made a little of it between tide and tide, it follows that the wave has to advance further than before to get right under the moon. It is exactly as if we placed the hour and minute hands of the clock, say at twelve. The minute hand will have to go more than once round before it overtakes the hour hand, as the latter will be slowly making its way towards the one o'clock. It is owing to this advance of the moon that the tides recur at intervals of about twelve hours and three-quarters. It is believed that the great tidal wave rises in the southern seas, where, every student of geography knows, there is the greatest area of ocean. There the tide is generally more equable in height, and regular in its occurrence, than in the northern hemisphere. It makes its way into the Atlantic and North Pacific, indenting the coast line, and adjusting its height to the geographical conditions it may meet with. How greatly these interfere with tidal effects may be seen by a consideration of the shapes and areas of the Atlantic and Pacific Oceans. Thus, the latter obtains its greatest breadth in an easterly and westerly direction; whilst in the former the longest diameter is in a northerly and southerly direction. Hence the great tidal wave, entering these vast oceans from the south, is instantly influenced by the form of the basins, or rather, it influences the currents. In the Pacific, we find that the currents are broad and slow, whilst in the Atlantic they are narrow and rapid. In the former, as a rule, the waves are low—in the latter they are high. It has been advanced recently, and by some of our best mathematicians, that the *drag* on the revolving of the earth on its axis, caused by the tides, must in the long run act as a break, so as to render the rate of revolution slower. In other words, to lengthen our days and nights. There can be little doubt that this is actually the case, and that, in some remote period, if the retardation goes on, it will end in the earth ceasing to revolve, or doing so at a much slower rate than at present. If this be the case, then, in the earlier geological epochs, the revolution of the earth on its axis must have been more rapid than at present; and this may have affected geographical changes, and even the conditions of animal and vegetable life, in a way of which we can now form no conception.

The waves or billows produced by these various disturbing agencies of tides, currents, and winds exercise a marvellous influence on the condition of the atmosphere. The force liberated as they dash over each other, or spend themselves against the shore, must be immense, and more than one earnest physical philosopher is turning his attention to the inquiry as to whether such force cannot be utilised for the service of mankind! We know that nothing is absolutely wasted—that the mechanical motion of the waves thus suddenly arrested is converted into heat, electricity, &c. One cannot wonder, therefore, that the sea-air should be distinguished for the peculiar character of its oxygen—that called *ozone*, which we know results from a remarkable electrical condition. It is this which inspires new life into the veins of the jaded holiday seeker, and which in fact makes the sea-air feel so exhilarating. The strength of the sea-waves is almost proverbially known. We are aware how the most powerful sea-walls, breakwaters, &c., give way before their constant battering. No rock is so hard that they cannot mechanically knock it to pieces and waste it away; whilst the softer portions of the coast-line are degraded with an almost inconceivable rapidity. Thus, the waste of the steeper parts of the Norfolk coast is reckoned at not less than three feet a year, and the coasts of Suffolk, Essex, Yorkshire, Hampshire, and elsewhere are, in some parts, being eaten away by the waves at nearly the same rate. Perhaps nothing affords us a better proof of the intense mechanical force of sea-waves than the ease with which they break up the strongest vessel after she has been stranded.

Out in the open sea these waves are most powerful. And yet, what few people imagine, their power does not extend downwards to any great depth. Off the coasts of Newfoundland is perhaps the place where the vertical depth of the waves extends most, and here it reaches to five hundred feet during a severe storm. The waves, in fact, are but commotions of the *surface* of the sea. The water itself does not shift, but the movements we call waves, which have been given to the water by the action of the wind, communicate this force to each other, and so pass it on until the last wave spends itself against the seashore. We can better understand it by observing the action of the wind on a field of wheat. We can see the breeze sweep over it, and notice the waves which bend down the brown ears, to rise again after the force has been removed. This waving of a wheat-field is exactly parallel to the rhythmical motion of the surface of the sea. The wheat itself does not move, nor does the body of the sea-water. When the wind is intermittent, as most ordinary breezes are, then the waves will run in for a short time, and be followed by a longer and higher ridge than the rest, which we may call the billow. This is simply due to the rhythmical fits and starts, and is to be noticed chiefly in fine weather—the waves being all tolerably equal as to height and length during a storm. When stormy winds have prevailed in one direction for a long time, by repeatedly pressing on the side of the wave they force it to bend over in the direction the wind is itself taking. Even this, however, is merely a rising and falling, an *oscillation*, of the water, in that particular place. The force of the storm-waves is indeed something terrible. Those of the Atlantic which break on the western coast of Ireland often run forty and fifty feet in height. Further, it is known that the velocity imparted to waves frequently attains the rate of a mile a minute. Single and unbroken waves have been observed coming in at this rate, whose body of water could not weigh less than two hundred tons. Can we wonder, when a projectile of this character dashes against the solid rocks, that we should feel the ground literally, and not figuratively, tremble beneath our feet? Along the Norfolk coasts, a north-west gale will strip off, in a single night, a deposit, twenty feet thick, of sand which has been accumulating for months. So much for the mechanical force of the waves, borrowed in the open sea, far away from land, from the gales which are perpetually pressing unevenly upon its surface, and piling the salt water into miniature mountains. But the pretty ripples which curl over in green, graceful curves, and gently run along the absorbing sands, owe that particular form to the friction in the shallow water. As the tide comes up, and gradually gains on the beach, the force with which it comes in is more or less retarded by the friction of the water on the sand. Thus the upper portion of the water being freer from this drawback, tends to run in more rapidly, and in doing so curls over and breaks in the manner we have mentioned.

We cannot do more, in the brief limits of our "Half-hour," than notice those marine phenomena to which allusion has already been made—the oceanic currents. We can hardly conceive the dreary, lifeless deserts of water our oceans and seas would be without this simple and beneficent arrangement. We know it for a fact that great bodies of water constantly move in different directions, and, in doing so, keep up a constant circulation. A few degrees of heat are alone sufficient to produce this marvellous result, aided, perhaps, in some cases, by the long-continued action of some such winds as the "trade winds." The general result is that the heat of the tropics causes a circulation of waters towards the poles, and the cold waters of these frigid regions creep along as bottom currents to replace them. Different depths of sea, contiguity of land, peculiarities of coast-line, and a hundred other disturbing elements, come in to produce a surprising variation, but the general and intended result is the same, nevertheless. Of all these currents, perhaps none is better known than the "Gulf Stream," so called because it takes its name from the Gulf of Mexico, whence it starts on its aquatic journey towards the poles. The revolution of the earth on its axis, fortunately for us, gives what would otherwise be a northerly current an easterly bias, and thus it impinges against British shores, warming the waters and the atmosphere resting on them to a considerable degree. To this agent, more than anything else, we owe the genial climate of the south and south-west of England and the west of Ireland, where its influence is most palpably felt. To it, also, is due the fact that Liverpool, although situated one degree more northerly than St. John's, Newfoundland, has always the Mersey open, whilst the latter trans-atlantic port is blocked up with ice nearly six months out of the year. The recent soundings of the "Porcupine" showed the important effects of these currents on marine life. It was found that where Arctic or cold currents ran along the ocean floor, notwithstanding that the upper waters were warmer, that floor was occupied by shell-fish similar to those living in the seas of the north. This great Arctic current is being more studied and better understood than formerly. What is true regarding an interchange of warm and cold waters in the northern hemisphere is equally so of those in the southern. The cold waters of the southern pole flow towards the equator in no fewer than three great currents. One of these splits up in forty-five degrees south latitude, sending one arm round Cape Horn, and the other, which is known as "Humboldt's Current," up the Chilian and Peruvian coasts. The second great southerly current runs towards Africa, getting divided by the Cape of Good Hope, so as to be forced up the eastern and western coasts. The hot water of the Indian Ocean escapes southerly, and is replaced by the third great current; so that the warm waters of the Indian Ocean circulate between Africa and Australia, one branch of the current running along the southern coast of the latter country.

These currents tend considerably to render the specific gravity of the sea-water tolerably equable, by mixing them up. In this they are aided by tides very considerably. For the ocean to maintain a tolerably equal specific gravity is of great importance to its animal life, especially when we remember the great depths which prevail in some parts of the sea. Formerly it was roughly estimated that the greatest depth of the ocean would be somewhere about that of the greatest height of our mountain chains. Some parts of the Pacific Ocean have been sounded, and no bottom felt at more than five miles. The Atlantic soundings for the cable showed that in many parts the depth was between two and three miles. It is now estimated that the average depth of the sea below, is more than *fifteen times* greater than the average height of the land above the sea-level. The seas and oceans of the globe occupy an area nearly three times greater than the land, having about one hundred and forty-eight millions of square miles of extent. To keep up the density of this mighty body, we have seen that a few currents, produced by the simplest causes, are more or less sufficient. Sea-water is known to contain nearly all the soluble salts and substances existing on the globe. This led a French geologist to hold that the present constituents of sea-water date from the earliest period of our globe's history. He says: " In the first stage of our planet, before the watery vapours contained in the primitive atmosphere were condensed, and before they had begun to fall on the earth in the form of boiling rain, the shell of the earth contained an infinite variety of heterogeneous mineral substances, some soluble in water, others not. When rain fell on the burning surface for the first time, the waters became charged with all the soluble substances, which were reunited and afterwards deposited, accumulating in the large depressions of the soil. The seas of the primitive globe were thus formed of rain-water, holding in solution all that the earth had given up, collected in large basins—chloride of sodium, sulphates of soda, magnesia, potassium, lime, and silicium, in the form of soluble silicate; in a word, every soluble matter that the primitive globe contained formed part of the mineral contingent of this water. If we reflect that through all time up to the present day none of the general laws of nature have changed—if we consider that the soluble substances contained in the water of the primitive seas have remained there, and that the fresh water of the rivers constantly replaces the water which disappears by evaporation—we have the true explanation of the *saltness* of the sea-water." This theory may seem ingenious, but it has undoubted good reasons for its support, and some of our best geological chemists are in favour of its being the only one that sufficiently accounts for the sea becoming and remaining salt. As far back as the Devonian period we have evidences of marine and fresh water action, relatively, in the organic remains of the rocks of that age—showing that salt water existed then as now, and was equally fit for the support of animal life. Farther back still, in the Cambrian epoch, we have evidences of tidal action in the *ripple marks* with which the upper surfaces of the rock layers are patterned.

Reference has already been made to the necessity for some such mighty reservoir of water as the ocean, for the fertilisation of the dry land. The fruitful showers which are constantly falling on the latter all originate in the sea. Before they find their way back again as rivers, what changes have they undergone! The fertilisation of the dry land can only be effected at the expense of a certain wear and tear of its surface. This is carried away by rivers and streams into the sea. The insoluble portion is mechanically precipitated, and forms sands and mudbanks—the soluble is distributed by tides, currents, &c., through the bulk of sea-water. Now, as the water raised by evaporation from the surface of the sea is absolutely pure, and as that returned to it by rivers is charged with various minerals, it follows that if there were no checks provided, the sea-water would gradually get denser and more saline. The *checks* are the animal and vegetable life-forms which crowd its waters, which are eternally dying and giving birth within its huge bulk, until the sea-water is, as Dr. Carpenter has well described it, "a kind of *weak* broth," from the decomposing animal matter dispersed through it. On this "weak broth" the lower forms of life live, sucking in the nourishment by mere contact and absorption. The other species prey on these, and thus the great chain of life extends upwards and onwards. Such minerals as carbonate of lime—most largely carried into the sea by all rivers—are utilised by the mollusca to form their shells with, by the corals to build up their reefs, and by the fishes to construct the bones of their skeletons. The much less quantity of silica finds its way into the frustrules of diatoms, the spicules of sponges, &c., and the iodine, silver, &c., are none the less necessary to the seaweeds on which thousands of marine species feed. Thus the quantity of mineral matter carried into the sea by rivers is exactly compensated for by the animals and plants which live there; it is quietly but surely stowed out of the way, the sea-water is kept in an equably pure condition, and always fit for animal life to be enjoyed in it—whilst, meantime, the accumulating shells of molluscs, the slowly forming reefs of coral, and the still more slowly collecting of the calcareous shells of foraminifera, are laying along the floors of existing seas the foundations of continents yet to be. Surely this must be esteemed by all right thinkers a marvellous means of getting over a present difficulty by making it insure a future benefit! Owing to this arrangement it is that in tropical regions, where the rainfall is greatest, the rivers the longest, the surface of the earth most worn and torn, and therefore where a larger quantity of mineral matter is carried into the sea than in temperate latitudes, the fish are larger, the coral-reefs peculiar to such districts, and the mollusca attain a weight of shell unknown elsewhere. In fact, the greater the difficulty, the

c

more striking the compensation which meets it. Even in its mechanical arrangement, therefore, we may see what a marvellous object these great waters are, and how little "Half an hour" can assist us in contemplating the great wonders which

" Rise to the swelling of the voiceful sea !"

## II.

### HALF AN HOUR WITH PREPARATIONS.

THE ardent and youthful student of zoology, bent on a week or two's recreation at the sea-side, will hardly be content with "Half an hour!" Judging from our own experience of days gone by, he will be "preparing" beforehand during a longer period than he can perhaps afford to stay. And yet there is a rich pleasure in the anticipations conjured up whilst thus "preparing." As he gets his odds and ends together, the holiday seeker is mean time imagining the bright sunny days he is about to give himself up to, and already he seems to feel the sea-breeze lifting his hair, and to hear the music of the waters rippling in his ear. His nostrils are filled, in fancy, with "the salt sea smell," and alas! sometimes this very anticipation exceeds reality.

We have always found one rule a good one in preparing for a few days' or weeks' zoologising by the sea-shore—to take as few things with us as possible, and to let our outfit and preparations be of the simplest and cheapest kind. It is foolish to burden one's self with *impedimenta* which shall be the means of infinite trouble in looking after whilst journeying, and of objurgation to "Mary Ann," the servant-of-all-work, when at our sea-side lodgings.

In fact, it is surprising what few things you actually require for the purposes we are describing, and how readily they may be obtained almost wherever you are going. Of course, there are one or two necessaries which are really such, and which we should advise you to take with you. Among these is a *microscope*. It need not be an expensive one, and, as we will suppose you to be a *young* beginner, with the usual characteristic of such, you may also be presumed to possess more expensive wishes than means, and therefore are *forced* to put up with an instrument of an inexpensive kind. But, if you intend to know anything of zoology, and especially of the habits, structures, &c., of the lower forms of animal life, a microscope you must have. You can just as well expect to be an astronomer without having a telescope, as to be a naturalist without a microscope. So far, therefore, please regard this useful instrument as an absolute necessity. We said that an expensive one was not required for sea-side recreations, and this is so, because as a rule you will only use low magnifying powers. In the evenings, and more especially on *wet* days, you will thank us for recommending you to take such a pleasant and profitable method of wiling away the time usefully.

Surely, your experience of sea-side visits must have included days when the sky was dark and lowering, and the rain came in fitful showers against the window panes. You remember getting up many times an hour, and craning your neck to detect signs of a change. The yellow and red-backed novel lost its attractions, for you felt that one of the holidays, which were so few in number, was slipping away without being enjoyed. The dismal wails of the German band at the end of the street seemed to be a requiem for the day you were losing, and you felt as if you could call out with the old Roman about it!

On days like these, dear reader, your microscope comes to you like a messenger of peace. You will be surprised to find how it enables you to economise your time. Perhaps for several days previously you had collected a heap of things, and placed them aside, intending to look at and examine them more closely by-and-by. That time has now come, and you set to work to utilise it. You examine, say, the spores of the seaweeds you have collected, the diatoms you have in that little bottle, or attempt for the first time to extract the tongue of a limpet or a whelk, for the purpose of seeing the rows of curved siliceous teeth that cover it. If you have brought with you a few slips of glass for "mounts," you may try your hand at mounting these objects, so that they remain for years useful mementoes of a pleasant visit.

Supposing you intend to "go in" for collecting anything you may come across, we should advise you to get a few, two or three, gardener's bell glasses, those usually known to that ancient craft as "propagators," Figs. 1, 2, 3. They may be had cheaply and easily enough, and any ordinary carpenter will soon make you stands for them to rest on. The following will give you a good idea of what we mean. You will also require a siphon for drawing

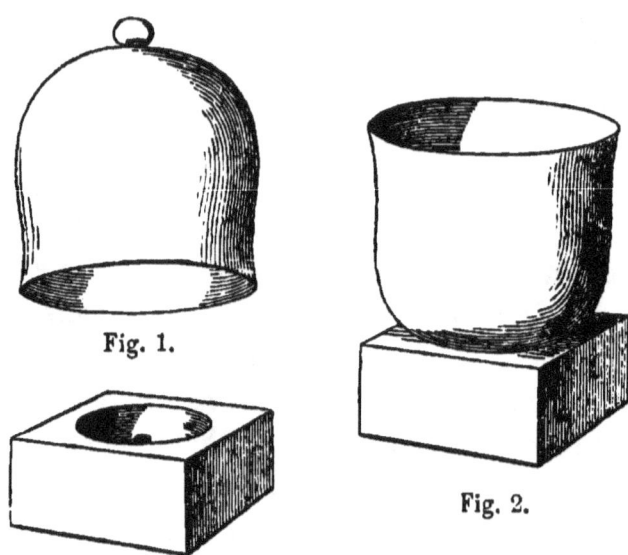

Fig. 1.

Fig. 2.

Fig. 3.

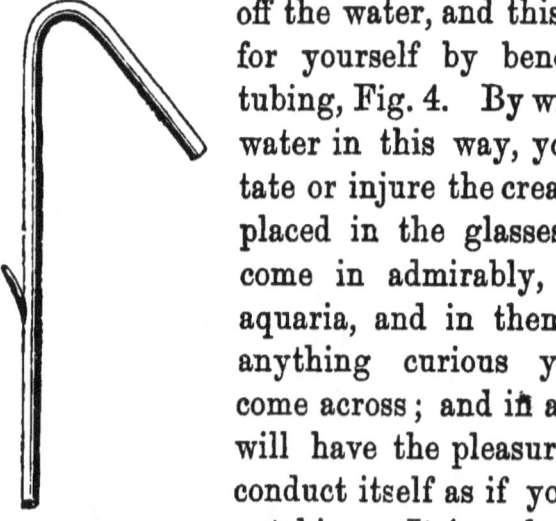

Fig. 4.

off the water, and this you can make for yourself by bending a bit of tubing, Fig. 4. By withdrawing the water in this way, you do not irritate or injure the creatures you have placed in the glasses. The latter come in admirably, as temporary aquaria, and in them you can drop anything curious you may have come across; and in a day or so you will have the pleasure of seeing it conduct itself as if you were not by watching. It is only by observing the habits of animals in this way, that you can thoroughly understand their structure, or perceive all their real beauties. And, as you may readily imagine, the task is anything but an unpleasant one, especially on one of the rainy days aforementioned. You require two or three separate glasses, because we will suppose you humane enough to prevent any undue massacre of their contents, as would be the case if you crowded all your "finds" into the same bowl. For instance, it would be as well to keep your anemones apart. They will look better, and present a very pretty sight, if you have been fortunate enough to secure several species, when they expand their tentacles and seem to be what popular fancy has dubbed them—"flowers of the sea."

Anemone collecting is always the most popular of any of the engagements of which we have been speaking, and we cannot wonder when we consider the beauty of the objects, especially after they have been kept in a bell-glass a day or two. But the task of obtaining them is not always the easiest or cleanest, although there is a spice of fun about it that perhaps seasons the attempt. We will suppose you have arrived at your destination, have hired your rooms, and are well satisfied with them, have got your bell-glasses and arranged them near the window, and all that you require now is to fill them. Of course, if the place you have selected be any well-frequented haunt, there will sure to be a guide-book, which, whatever may be its natural history veracity, will also be certain to give you some information as to the marine animals to be met with in the neighbourhood. You are thankful for any assistance, no matter from what source it may come, and you make yourself acquainted with what the local guide-book, or if there be one of a more certain character, with what these have to say as to habitats, &c, and act accordingly. It is not wise to throw away any hint when you are at the sea-side, as you wish to economise your time, and to crowd into your too-limited stay as much enjoyment and information as you can.

A botanical vasculum is a capital thing to throw over your shoulders, and, with a basket containing a hammer and chisel, one or two small, but wide-mouthed bottles, a walking-stick, and a net whose hoop will double up so as to go into the basket or pocket, and contrived to fit on to the end of your stick, are all you will require. You may think these amply sufficient, and so they are; but we cannot see how you can do with less. As to your dress, that is a subject best left to yourself; only, as a rule, the strongest and oldest will look better after your morning's work, than if you had gone out kid-gloved and fashionably dressed. If you are wise, you will see specially to your *boots*, that they be thick-soled and hob-nailed. There is a popular and mistaken tradition current that you cannot take cold with salt water, as if there were no dampness in it. All we can say is, don't try the experiment on yourself. Of course we will suppose the morning on which you make your first expedition is fine and bracing. The sun shines brightly, and the sea breeze tempers its heat to a delicious warmth. The waves come in in long dazzling ripples, and break on the pebbly strand with a murmur that seems sweetest music to your enraptured sense. You stand still a moment to drink in the scene, and to allow its effects to have their full influence. Yesterday, perhaps, you were in London or some other large town, longing for change and rest after a year's toil, as the "hart panteth for the waterbrooks!" To-day you have thrown business aside, and you have gone back in life ten or twenty years with the sudden change. It is wonderful the effect! We take too few holidays, and make too little of them, or we should be, some of us, better and wiser men!

Away, in the distance, about a mile, perhaps, is a jutting headland, whose form tells you that rockpools may be expected to be found there. To this you make your way, for these are the choice zoological collecting places for shore objects. As you walk along, your eyes are well directed to the beach, where you may pick up several species of shells, especially after a windy night, and where the stronger seaweeds, which have been uprooted by the waves, are strewn. About the roots of the latter you may find some valuable specimens of foraminifera, &c., for your microscope, which you can place in your bottle to examine another time. On the fronds of these large seaweeds, also, you will find several species of zoophytes attached, many of which may be still alive. Pieces of these algæ are torn off, and immersed in one of your larger bottles, so that, when you get home, you may transfer your treasures to one of your bell-glasses, and have the pleasure, in an hour or two, to see the battered zoophytes expanding their delicate cups, as if grateful for the rescue. Having arrived at the headland, you see that your expectations are not deceived, for here are rock-pools in plenty, and of varying depth, so that you may expect good sport. Bending over them, presently your eyes get accustomed to the dim light, and you are able to peer into the smallest corner of the pool, and notice its most inconspicuous inhabitant. The spot seems like a fragment of fairyland, with its living sea-firs, its delicately-tinted purple and green seaweeds, its gorgeous anemones with spread tentacles, and, darting here and there, the small fishes peculiar to these habitats. Meantime you see the *gammarus*, perhaps followed by its brood of young, as chickens will follow the hen; or a sly old crab is making his way sidelong, his stalked eyes directed towards yourself. Here is good ground for anemone hunting, and having laid down your book, you set to work with hammer and chisel to detach the rock on which these lovely objects are attached. This is the only way of obtaining them, and you have to be very careful in doing it, so as not to injure the *base* of the animal—its only vulnerable part. Hammering away, of course your transparent rock-pool is soon converted into a filthy, muddy puddle; and you may depend upon it, its tenants, who may have occupied it for generations, are in no small stew as to what is the matter. Before you disturbed the water, you saw a good ledge where you could place the point of your chisel, and you knew you had only to keep it here to detach the fragment of rock, with the anemone attached to it. It was well you noticed this, as you cannot see anything after you have given a few blows, and you are obliged to feel for the anemone (which has long ago drawn in its tentacles, and is silently awaiting its fate). Every now and then an ill-directed blow splashes your face with salt water, and your eyes smart with the unusual and unexpected application. At length perseverance is rewarded, for the last blow has detached the piece of rock, and perhaps your hand has slipped and got scratched. Taking little or no notice of this—for it is what you may expect, and therefore what you may, in a great measure, guard against—you grope along the bottom until you find the specimen. Can that insignificant, ugly lump of jelly adhering to it, be the brightly-coloured creature whose tentacles made it appear like some gorgeous flower? Yes, such it is, and such anemones will always look after rough usage like that your particular specimen has just undergone. However, you bottle it, and, when you return, you place it and others you may have obtained, in a separate bell-glass, with fresh sea-water. It will perhaps be a day or two before they have got over their change, and you must not be surprised even if you see them lying inert at the bottom of the glass. But after a few days your patience will be rewarded, and your extemporised aquarium be converted into a living garden.

A hammer and chisel will be equally useful to you should you see any *Pholades* imbedded in the rocks, and comfortably ensconced in the holes they have excavated in a way it still puzzles many naturalists to understand. To obtain the portion of rock in which a specimen is lodged, is rather a difficult process; and you must expect the well-directed siphon of the animal to aim a jet or two of water at your eyes whilst you are endeavouring to dislodge it, or rather, to carry it away, lodgings and all. The same implements will further be found handy supposing you come across some sponge adherent to the rock, which you wish to take home that you may study its habits, and watch the currents it will make in your aquarium. All this, to say nothing about geological specimens which may strike your eye, and tempt your hand! Mean time your net will have come in handy to sweep the rock-pools for minute crustacea or fish, or to enable you to reach objects which it would have been impossible to have secured else.

A few mornings spent in this manner will have furnished you with objects enough, and have given you a good idea of the littoral zoology of the neighbourhood. To vary your amusement as well as your study, you may desire to have a sail, an engagement which, depend upon it, you have already been solicited about by the amphibious-looking boatmen, who eye your studies with hardly concealed contempt, and pass their own satire and small jokes upon them. Extend your sail over a few hours, morning or afternoon, only, if possible, select a time when the tide is flowing, not ebbing. A great many objects of interest and value may be obtained by your using a towing-net, Fig. 5, let out behind your boat. This is a capital method of getting the jelly-fish, &c.,

Fig. 5.

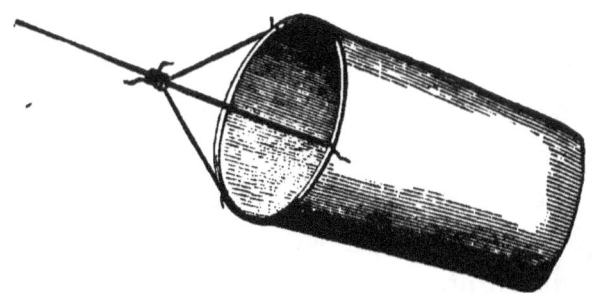

Major Holland's home-made Towing-net.

creatures which otherwise you will only meet with in the stranded and half-putrifying condition. The construction of a towing-net is a very easy task, and its outlay very inexpensive. Get a child's wooden hoop, about two feet in diameter, at some toy shop. Next procure some strong, coarse linen, a yard wide, and a few yards of sash-line. Fold the cloth in the middle, so as to bring the two ends together, and then sew up the sides, stitching them outside. Place the wooden hoop outside the bag, and turn the edges of the latter well over it, so as to cover it completely. Then sew it close and tight all round, so that the bag may hang free from the lower inner edge of the hoop. Next cut the sash-line in two, laying the pieces evenly side by side: take them both together exactly in the centre, and letting the four ends hang down, make an overhand knot of all parts, five or six inches below the bend. This will give you a loop, or rather, two precisely equal loops, above the one knot. The four pendent ends you put through four little holes in the bag, placed at equal distances from each other, and then close up under the hoop, passing the ends from inside, bringing them up over the outside of the hoop, and securing each one to its own part by a double stitch. If this be done properly and carefully, the hoop will be exactly horizontal and evenly balanced, and you will have provided yourself with a capitally strong net for about eighteen pence. Let the boat get about half a mile away from the beach before you throw it over, towing it about ten feet astern. If you are sailing or rowing at the rate of about three or four miles an hour, you will then be able to keep about half the hoop above the surface, and thus prevent the larger captives making their escape. Supposing you have made a moonlight excursion—a capital season for zoologising—you may reckon on getting some good finds by the method above described. After you have towed the net about ten minutes or a quarter of an hour, you examine its contents, dropping them one by one into the basin or bottle which you have brought with you, so that you may examine them at greater detail when you return.

Another capital plan of studying deeper sea life, is to get up early, so that you may be on the jetty when the trawl-boats come in. The "rubbish," as the sailor calls it, consists of hosts of creatures which the dredge has brought up, often much mangled and defaced, from the bottom of the sea. You pick the best, and place them in one of your bell-glasses, and in a day or two they will reward you for your pains. Or, if you "tip" the trawl-boatmen as they are going out, so that they may put all the "rubbish" in a bucket specially for you, then you may anticipate a capital harvest. A little beer goes a great way with these men, and they are always pleased, besides, if you take any interest in things that live in the sea. If you can stand the pitching and tossing, the wet and the cold, and are thoroughly proof against sea-sickness; if you are proof against the vile smells that reek in trawl-boats, compounds of pitch, rum, bacon, and fish; then bribe the captain to let you go with them for a night! If you can bear all we have described, and a good deal more it is impossible to describe, you will come into contact with

## 32  HALF AN HOUR WITH PREPARATIONS.

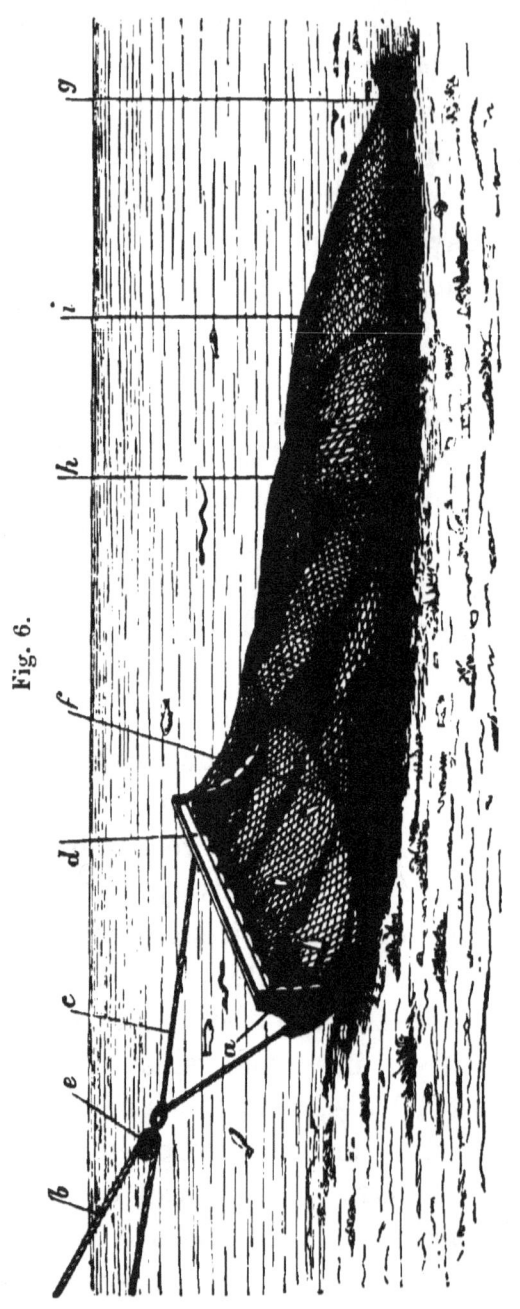

Fig. 6. — The Trawl.

facts in a way you will never forget. Indeed, there is nothing like a night or two's outing with the trawl-boats for introducing you to marine zoology. The following is the principle on which that useful object, the trawling-net, is constructed. There is a large iron head (*a*) attached to a beam, as in the accompanying Figure 6. To the latter the net is fastened, its end terminating in what is called a "cob," or end of the bag of the net, in which there is a large opening through which the contents of the net can be taken out. Supposing the above to be a prawn trawl, then it will be about seven feet wide at the mouth, and about fifteen feet in length. The "head" has two heavy iron plates, not much unlike the runners of sledges. These support the beam, and skid along the bottom. The lower part of the net is fastened to what is called the "ground rope," which is always a couple of feet behind the upper part, so that when the fish rise, being alarmed by its sweeping over where they lie, they are stopped by the upper part, and then swept into the body of the net by the speed at which the boat is sailing. It follows, therefore, that all moving living things lying on the sea bottom will be introduced into the net, so that its zoological contents are often of a very varied description.

Our intending sea-side student is now in as full possession of the necessary "preparations" as, if applied, cannot fail to result in a harvest of objects it will take him weeks to study. We wish him health, feeling certain he will find pleasure for himself. All the better for him if he can find a friendly spirit for a companion, one who can enter into the necessary interest of the objects sought after. Alas! the time will fly away only too soon, and the much-looked for holiday be over, almost before you seem to have begun it. But you will have gained bodily and intellectually, and return home a better and a wiser man than when you left.

## III.

#### HALF AN HOUR WITH SEAWEEDS.

It may have occupied you, gentle reader, the whole morning, in collecting the treasures to which we are about to devote half an hour's gossip. To be successful in collecting seaweeds, you ought to follow the retreating tide step by step. When it has reached its farthest, then you may expect to be rewarded, especially if the sea bottom be rocky and uneven. There is nothing like broken ground for studying the marine flora. As you have walked along you have been surprised at the marvellous abundance of seaweeds of every size and colour, occupying nearly every available patch of the area.

A rich meadow in June does not bring forth a more charming variety of grasses and flowers than does the rocky ground between high and low tides. Your vasculum speedily gets filled, to say nothing of the monsters as tall as yourself, which the most enthusiastic botanist would never dream of "mounting." All that you can do with them is to examine them, to cut off such portions as are interesting, say the fructifying organs ; or examine them carefully for the rich store of zoophytes, parasitic seaweeds, &c., usually attached to them. Supposing you to have exhausted a collecting ground like this, you may add still further to your list by taking a boat, and dragging the bottom with a clawed drag. Much the same difference occurs with the marine flora as the terrestrial. Height above the sea-level materially influences the distribution of the genera and species on land, and *depth* does the same with seaweeds below it. Those who wish to study the general laws which regulate this apportionment of animal and vegetable life, are referred to Professor Edward Forbes's theory of the zones of depth which belt every island and mainland.

Seaweeds are roughly, but sharply, divided into three distinct groups, according to the colour of their spores, which are black (or olive), red, and green. The names given to these are Melanosperms, Rhodosperms, and Chlorosperms. Minor, but important subdivisions again occur, based upon the peculiar character of the spores themselves. We will take the black or olive group of seaweeds first, as they are most abundant, as well as strongest and largest. Indeed, these latter qualities enable them completely to monopolise the ground in many instances, to the complete exclusion of diminutive species, which are forced in self defence often to become parasitic on their more powerful neighbours. In this respect, therefore, their smallness may actually be advantageous to them. We have spoken of such species as *parasitic*, but this must not be understood in the sense in which we understand parasitism in terrestrial plants. Properly speaking, seaweeds have no real roots, nor do they need any, as they do not draw their nutriment from the earth, but from the sea water. The smaller seaweeds have no appearance of roots at all, and, in the larger, you will readily see that the fibrils of the stem, which look like roots, are in reality only a kind of clasper, to get firm hold of the rocks by. Their usual mode of anchoring or attaching themselves is by a sort of disk. This is seen more especially in the *chorda filum*, or "sea-cord," an object you cannot fail to have recognised in the dark olive, almost black, round, cord-like weed, perhaps many feet in length, which lay entwined among other seaweeds. This particular weed often reaches the length of twenty to forty feet.

By far the commonest of these "black" spored seaweeds is that group popularly known as "sea-wracks," which you may see lying in dark, unattractive heaps at low water. First, there is the "black tang," or "bladder-wrack" (*Fucus vesiculosus*), whose long fronds are often two feet in length. These fork repeatedly into what we may call branches, each having a stout mid-rib running down the centre, and covered with warty tubercles, or bladders, arranged in pairs (Fig. 7). The presence of this mid-rib distinguishes the species *vesiculosus* from the nearly allied species *nodosus*, in which the mid-rib is altogether absent. The "bladders," to which we have referred, are hollow, and filled with air, so as to render the weed buoyant in the water. It is a common practical joke with sea-side boatmen, to persuade youngsters to place such bladdered seaweeds on the fire, telling them some tale or another to encourage them to do so; but well aware of the volleys of explosions that will occur if their advice

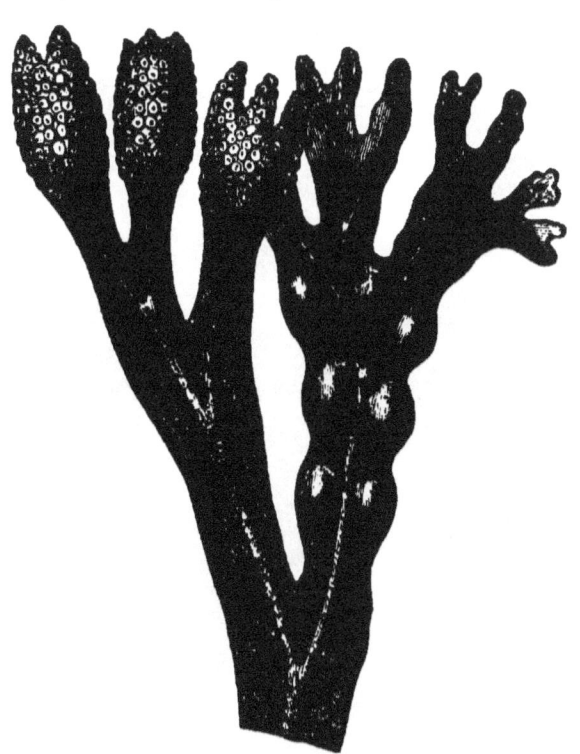

Black Tang, or Bladder-wrack (*Fucus vesiculosus*).

be carried out. The tips of the fronds or "branches" of these "wracks" will sometimes appear swollen, and covered with little tubercles scarcely raised above the surface. These contain the arrangement for the fructification of the plant, which is exceed-

38    HALF AN HOUR WITH SEAWEEDS.

ingly curious, and well worth a little further consideration. Each of the little frustrules has a minute opening, through which their contents escape.

Fig. 8.

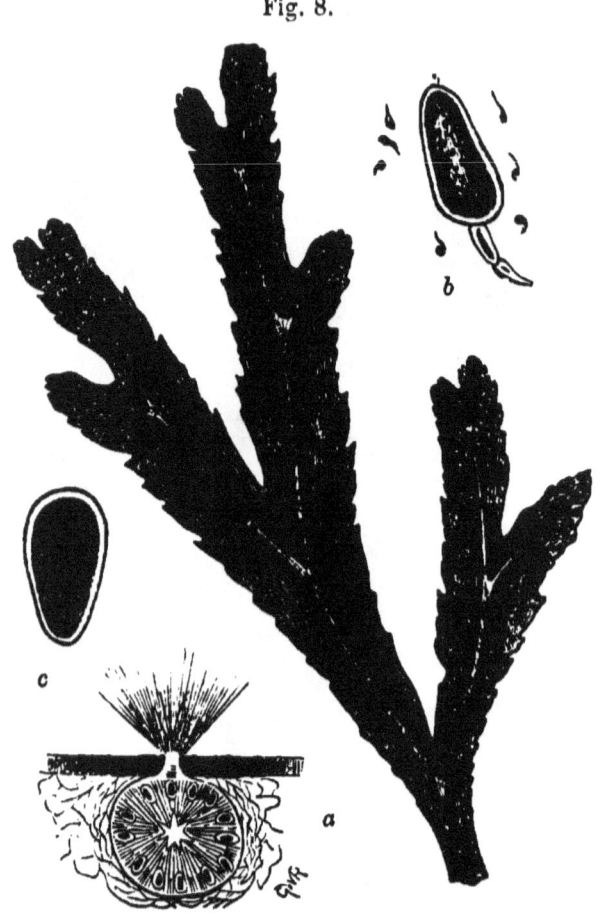

Serrated Wrack (*Fucus serratus*).

If we cut one of these tips or tubercles across, then each frustrule will be seen representing a cell or internal cavity, enclosing, in one plant, what are called *antheridia*, and, in another, the *spores* (see

Fig. 8, *a*). The former are usually regarded as the *male*, and the latter as the *female* organs. In every case, both are produced on separate plants. The *antheridia* are little bags containing small bodies called *zoospores* (*b*). These no sooner escape in the way mentioned, than they move about in the water as if they were little animals, and not plants at all. The *spores* are little grains of an oblong shape, which ultimately separate into a certain number of parts (*c*). These perform the functions of seeds, which are fertilised by the zoospores, just as the ovules are by the pollen of flowering plants. The serrated wrack (*Fucus serratus*) resembles the *vesiculosus* in its general form, but it may at once be distinguished by its having no air-bladders, and by the edges of the fronds being serrated. Like the former, its fruit is borne at the tips of the fronds. Indeed, this species is usually recommended as the best for microscopical examination of the phenomena we have been describing. Professor Harvey advises that fresh specimens should be collected in winter or early spring, and, being removed from the water, that they should be left till they were partially dry. As the surface dries there will exude from the pores of the receptacle drops of a thick orange-coloured fluid, which, on being placed under a microscope and moistened with salt water, will be seen to be composed of innumerable cellules, from which will issue troops of these atoms. No sooner are they liberated, than they commence those singular zoosporic motions which naturalists have found so difficult to reconcile with vegetable life. The species of "sea-wrack," however, that is best known, especially for the explosive power of its bladders when treated in the manner aforesaid, is the "knotted wrack" (*Fucus nodosus*, Fig. 9). In this species the receptacles which form the fructification are not terminal, as in that just mentioned, but are borne in stalks or pedicels issuing from either side of the fronds. In the "knotted wrack," also, the spore separates into *four*, whence their name of *tetraspores* (Fig. 9 *a*). In the "serrated wrack," however, these spores divide into *eight* parts, called sporules. Another kind of wrack, nearly as well known as the above, is the *Fucus canaliculatus*, having fronds only a few inches in length, and the spores separated into *two* spores (see Fig. 10 *a*). Besides the above, there are two or three

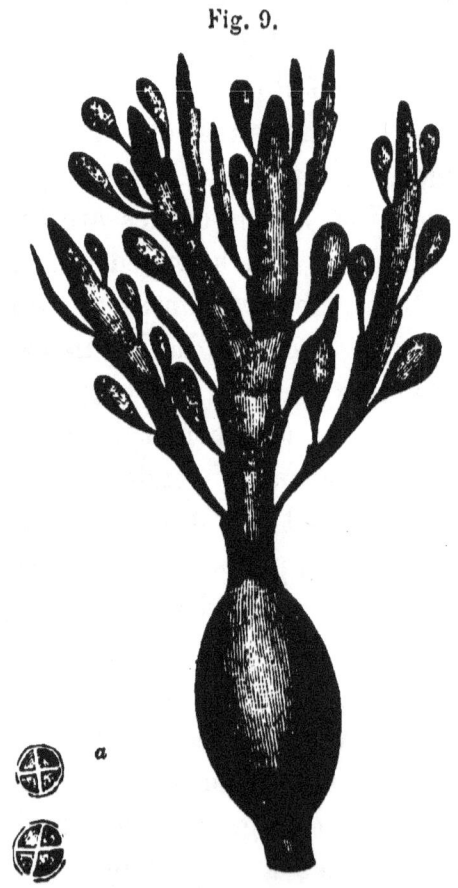

Knotted Wrack (*Fucus nodosus*).

other species of Fucus, of a less common occurrence. The word "wrack," it may be observed, is derived from the French *varec*, which signifies a seaweed.

After a storm, you will scarcely fail to see strewn on the beach, just above high-water mark, a seaweed with a long thick stem of three or four feet,

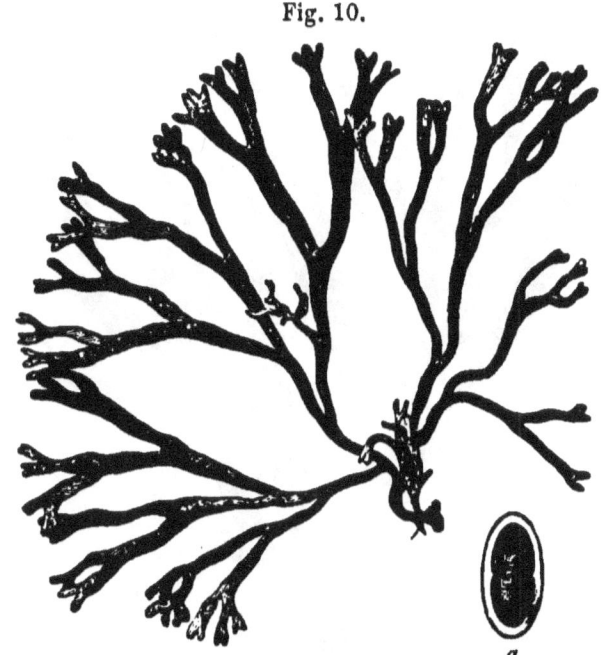

Fig. 10.

Small Wrack (*Fucus canaliculatus*).

and having its leaves or fronds digitate, or separating from a common base, just like the fingers of the human hand. This is the *Laminaria digitata*. An allied and almost equally common species, distinguished by the greater length of its fronds, is *L. saccharina*. After this weed has been lying in the sun for a few hours, it becomes more or less covered with a hoar-frost-like substance, which is sweet, and resembles the "mannite" sold in chemists' shops, hence the name of the species. The stems of the two latter are tough, and become hard when dried, so that it is not uncommon to see portions

Fig. 11.

*Halidrys siliquosa*, nat. size.

turned into fork handles, the prong of the fork being inserted when the portion was soft, and recently cut off.

On various parts of the rocks, during your rambles, you may have observed a little, bushy-tufted, olive-coloured seaweed, called *Halidrys siliquosa* (Fig. 11).

It takes its name from two Greek words signifying "oak-tree." It possesses bladders, or air-vessels, which in shape resemble pods, hence its specific name of *siliquosa*. This species is very common on the Welsh coasts, and everywhere it is a favourite with the naturalist, on account of the numerous small zoophytes, &c., it harbours among its dense fronds.

The *Rhodosperms* comprehend the most beautiful of all species of seaweeds, and hence they are most sought after by collectors, and for ornamental purposes. Their tints of scarlet and red are of various shades, and the group includes species whose fronds are not red at all. Nearly every species grows submerged, and a large number of them in deep water. The latter, therefore, can only be obtained by dredging, or after a storm has uprooted them and cast them ashore. Even then, unless you be fortunate enough to gather them soon after they have been cast up, they will be almost worthless for herbarium purposes, on account of their being soon acted upon by the sun, so as to lose their bright colours. On the stems of *Laminaria*, above-mentioned, we may find the peculiar dark-red *Polysiphonia urceolata*, whose jar-shaped fruits are very pretty objects when seen through a low magnifying power. The *Chlylocladia articulata*, also, is a good specimen to mount, because of the readiness with which it adheres. This can easily be identified by the *jointed* branches, whence its specific name. Unfortunately, however, it soon fades, even in the herbarium, but it remains a pretty object nevertheless. In the little rock-pools you will notice the sides frequently covered with a red, limy incrustation. This is the base of the coralline seaweed (*Corallina officinalis*, Fig. 12), a little plant of great interest, and long believed to belong to the animal kingdom, on account of the quantity of carbonate of lime it secretes. It soon bleaches, and then assumes a tint of dirty whiteness. Other algæ are now known which have the same power of secreting lime, among which are the genera *Jania, Acetabularia, Liagora,* and *Melobesia*. Perhaps one of the most beautiful of the *Rhodosperms* is the *Delesseria sanguinea*, whose specific name greatly assists in its identification. Its colour is of the most beautiful scarlet, and you may further learn to distinguish it by its midrib and distinct nervures. Few objects look better in the herbarium, as it dries well without losing its colour, and its mucus acts as a natural gum and causes it to adhere firmly. The *Ptilota plumosa* is another beautiful red seaweed, whose feather-like fronds will assist you in identifying it. The stiffer, bristle-like fronds of *Griffithsia setacea* are worth notice, and you will hardly fail to find it growing in the darker crannies of the rock-pools. When a newly-gathered specimen is placed in fresh water, the membrane bursts, and the red colouring

Fig. 12.

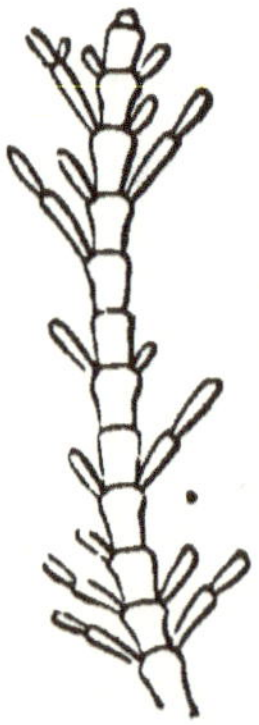

Corallina officinalis (mag.).

matter is shot out. A common, but not obscure seaweed, is the "Dulse," *Rhodymenia palmata* (Fig. 13), so called from its palmate form. This is an

Fig. 13.

*Rhodymenia palmata.*

edible weed, and capable of being cooked. The fronds of the *Porphyra laciniata* much resemble the common green laver, except that they are of a bright scarlet. They are so thin that they cling to your fingers like a film when you attempt to lift them out of the water, and they give the young beginner infinite trouble in his endeavours to arrange them in his herbarium. Abundant in almost every rock-pool you will find the *Plocamium coccineum* (Fig. 14), a weed with a beautiful crimson hue, which, as usual, soon fades, and ultimately subsides into a dirty white.

Fig. 14.

*Plocamium coccineum.*

Occasionally you may stumble across a rarity or two, such as the "Peacock," or "Turkey-feather" laver (*Padina pavonia*), growing where it can enjoy the full light and heat of the sun. This is one of the most charming of all our seaweeds, and from its varying tints well deserves the name of "Peacock." *Nitophyllum punctatum* is also a handsome plant, which can easily be distinguished from the Delesseria, to which it bears some resemblance, by the absence of a mid-rib. Its colour is of a delicate crimson hue. The "Carrageen," or "Irish" moss (*Chondrus crispus*, Fig. 15), is well known from its supposed medicinal powers. Although it is included among the Rhodosperms, it is often of a pale greenish colour. It grows in large masses, and is one of our commonest weeds. When washed and boiled down into a jelly, flavoured with lemon, it is said to be very pleasant.

Fig. 15.

Carrageen (*Chondrus crispus*).

The black or olive-coloured seaweeds may be distinguished for their size, and the red for their beauty, but there can be no doubt that the green (*Chlorosperms*) are by far the most abundant. You can hardly stir at low water without noticing meadows of a fine, thread-like seaweed mantling every stone and piece of rock with its dark, almost sap-green. This is the *Enteromorpha compressa*, a plant capable of great variation in the shape and size of its fronds. All the true green seaweeds are notorious for their power of secreting oxygen, and this peculiarity must be of great value to the marine animals, which find at once a protection and invigoration amid their dense fronds. This oxygen-forming power is especially noticeable in the common green laver (*Ulva latissima*), hence its value in the marine aquarium. Very abundant almost everywhere the young collector will find *Cladophora rupestris* and *C. arcta*; the former a coarse, horsehair sort of seaweed, and the latter a trifle prettier. But by far the most graceful and elegant of the Melanosperms is the pretty little *Bryopsis plumosa*, not a common plant, and one which, once seen, will be always remembered afterwards. Its specific name of "feathery" is a capital description of its general appearance.

"How to mount seaweeds," so as to make them present something of their original beauty as seen when their delicate fronds were waving in the water, is a very important and sometimes difficult problem to the young collector. The best method is first to separate the specimens, and then to lay each on the edge of a plate in which there is water. They should not be placed in the water, however, but just on the side, so that they may imbibe sufficient moisture during the next operation without being actually immersed. Then take a piece of stiff drawing-paper and push it under the water slowly and carefully, so as to prevent air-bubbles forming on the surface, otherwise the subsequent treatment will cause the paper to be raised into folds and wrinkles. Having prepared the paper to receive your seaweeds, next draw the latter gently over it, with the root-end towards yourself. Then, by means of a smooth, blunt needle, you will be able to keep the stem and fronds from being entangled. Here you will be obliged to use your own experience and judgment as to their natural position, and the angle at which they ramified from each other when living. The large branches should be laid out in this manner first, after which proceed to arrange the minor ones. If this process be done deliberately and without precipitation, the tiniest and smallest of the branches and filaments may be arranged in their proper places. No fingers are so well fitted for this delicate operation as those of a lady, and we have never yet seen seaweeds whose arrangement for skill and taste could compare with those of the gentler sex. But when carefully mounted and properly named, few objects look better, or are fitter for presents. To look over an album of well and neatly-arranged seaweeds is a genuine treat, and even the most indifferent admirer of nature will here be forced to pay his tribute of admiration. There is something great as well as pretty in the presence of these "flowers of the sea." Just as the land vegetation exhales the gas absolutely necessary to terrestrial animals, and, at the same time, furnishes them with food, so do these seaweeds secrete that oxygen without which the swarming myriads of marine life would die of asphyxiation; taking up, meantime, the carbonic acid, absorbing it into their tissues, and thus turning it into the solid, nutritious, and in many cases the only food obtainable by them.

> " Ever drifting, drifting, drifting,
> On the shifting
> Currents of the restless main;
> Till in sheltered coves, and reaches
> Of sandy beaches,
> All have found repose again."
> LONGFELLOW.

## IV.

### HALF AN HOUR WITH SPONGES.

How very few people have any idea of what a sponge really is! Their total knowledge of it is, that it is something to wash with. Of its being an animal—or rather a colony of animals—they can form no conception. A live sponge is as different from the dried, spongy thing commonly called a sponge, as any two objects could be. It is only within the last few years that the animal nature of this organism has been thoroughly proved, and even yet there are not wanting people who regard sponges as something half-way between animals and plants. All true naturalists, however, are now convinced as to the exact position which these objects ought to hold in the animal kingdom.

Allow us to introduce you to a real, live sponge, such a one as you may dredge up from tolerably deep water off our own coasts. Unfortunately British sponges are neither common nor striking objects, and few collectors would care to trouble themselves much about them. But if you have a microscope, and want objects for it, you cannot do better than study our native sponges, and obtain the variously-shaped spicules from them. Supposing you can get living sponge, such as *Chalina oculata*, Fig. 25, what do you perceive? That the substance to which you have always given the name of *sponge*, is only the skeleton, in reality, of the entire animal. Inside the large and small openings, and outside the whole skeleton, is a gelatinous substance resembling white of egg, which is sometimes faintly coloured. This is the real "sponge flesh." It frequently has distributed through it minute spicules, as if for support; whilst these spicules interlace, and, with the horny fibre, make up the body of the skeleton—that which when dried always goes by the name of "sponge." When this gelatinous flesh, commonly called *sarcode*, is examined, it is seen to possess a granular structure. These grains very much resemble the simple organism —one of the very lowest in the animal kingdom —which is common in stagnant ponds, the little *Amœba*. In fact, the "sponge-flesh" may be regarded as a colony of these amœboid animals united together, just as a coral reef is composed of a colony of zoantharians. You will observe that both in this gelatinous exterior and the internal skeleton there are certain openings, large and small. In the species we have mentioned—the commonest thrown ashore after a storm—you see the larger orifices running in rows down each branch (see Fig. 25). Of these two kinds of perforations, the larger are termed "oscula," and the smaller go by the commoner name of "pores." The former are "exhalent," that is, they throw out wasted matter and excreted food; whilst the "pores" are "inhalent," suck in and absorb. Simple though this "sponge-flesh" appears to be, and really is, it is nevertheless provided with a simple means by which it can keep up a constant and beautiful circulatory system of sea-water throughout its entire structure. Inside the sponge are a series of chambers communicating directly with the external "pores." These are all lined with the *sarcode*, or "sponge-flesh," and here we find the granules ciliated, that is, having hair-like processes formed by a simple prolongation of the gelatinous tissue. These cilia keep up a constant agitation, and by so doing create currents in the water, which, passing through, nourish every individual particle, and after doing so, pass out by means of the "oscula." As Professor Huxley has well remarked, the whole sponge represents "a kind of subaqueous city, where the people are arranged about the streets and roads in such a manner, that each can easily appropriate his food from the water as it passes along." Sponges are reproduced by the detachment of little gemmules, or sarcode particles, which pass into the open sea through the "oscula" aforementioned. When first thrown off, each gemmule is furnished with cilia, by means of which it moves about until it finds a convenient spot where it can settle down into a sober sponge like its ancestors.

Sponges are among the oldest organisms of our globe, for we find several genera fossilised in the Silurian rocks. They are capable of being divided into three great groups, according to the nature of their framework or skeleton. We have spoken of the spicules, or needle-shaped crystals, which enter so largely into the structure of this skeleton, and are also found dispersed through the sarcode. Well, these spicules differ very considerably in their mineral nature, some being composed of lime, and others of silex. This difference at once indicates a difference in the animals capable of secreting the two minerals. And yet we are totally in the dark as to how either is secreted. The three divisions referred to are the *Keratose, Silicate,* and *Calcareous.* The first includes all the sponges whose framework is of a *horny* texture, as in the common washing sponge. This group, however, merges in both the others by occasionally having lime and silex spicules dispersed through it. You would find it difficult enough to wash with a genuine silicated sponge! Indeed, it requires to be handled as gently as possible, otherwise the fine, needle-shaped spicules will pierce the skin unawares, and produce an irritation for a long time afterwards. The silicated sponges include the most highly organised and ornamental of the

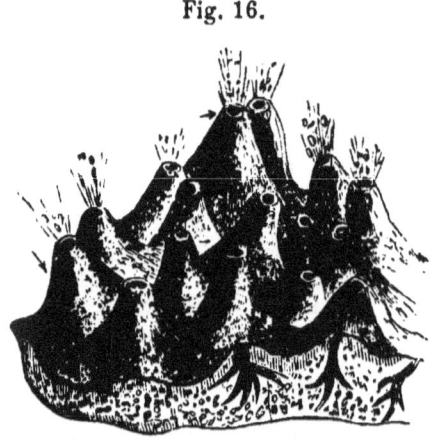

Fig. 16.

Osculæ of Sponge.

HALF AN HOUR WITH SPONGES. 55

Fig. 17.

whole family, as any one who has seen the "Venus's Flower Basket" (*Euplectella*), or even the "Glass-rope Sponge" (*Hyalonema*), Fig. 17, will readily admit. The latter sponge, which has for a long time been thought peculiar to the Japanese seas, has recently been dredged up off the coasts of Portugal. The silicated sponges frequently have a continuous siliceous fibre, as in the "roots" of Fig. 17, whose glass-like appearance has given the name to the sponge. The spicules in this species are both very beautiful and various, including a number of shapes and sizes. It will be seen that the "head" of the sponge presents the usual appearance by which we know these particular organisms. The following are three of the most marked of these pretty spicules, Figs. 18, 19, 20.

The calcareous sponges have their framework composed of carbonate of lime. This group

*Hyalonema mirabilis*, ¼ nat. size.

appears to be the oldest, having been found in the formations just mentioned. They were very abundant during the Cretaceous epoch, including those elegant fossils known as "Choanites" and *Ventriculites*.

Our British sponges belong to the horny (or *keratose*) and the calcareous groups. As we have already remarked, those living at low water are very small and insignificant, their bright colours alone rescuing them from utter contempt. To find them, you must go to where the rocks jut out furthest to sea; and here, at low water, you will see in the upper parts of the miniature caverns which may be formed in them,

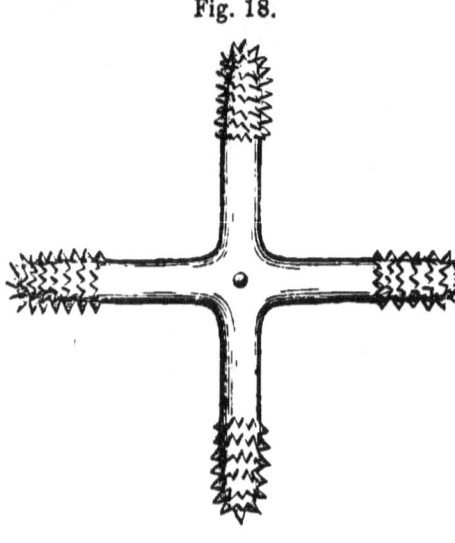

Fig. 18.

Mag. × 200.

Fig. 19.

Mag. × 100.

and in the darkest corners, certain patches of red and orange. They are seldom or never more than an inch in thickness, frequently nothing like that, and exactly resemble coloured lichens. Among the species you are likely to come across, we may mention two belonging to the genus *Grantia coriacea* and *compressa*. The former is a bright vermilion-coloured patch of soft but dense substance, about an inch in diameter only. The surface is covered by a series of small orifices—the *oscula*, to which we have referred. When dead, this sponge turns to the colour of a dried leaf, but when alive it is covered by a layer of firm sarcode, or "sponge-flesh," which gives it a peculiar feel when handled. Both these species of Grantia possess spicules, most of which are three-rayed (see Fig 21). Perhaps in the same cavern or hollow you may find a larger species (*Halichondria incrustans*), which, as its name implies, is incrusting the rock with its thick, undulating surface, which is slightly raised into pap-like ridges, and covered with shallow, winding sinuses. On the top of each of these ridges are the mouths, or "oscula." The whole sponge may be several inches in diameter, and about three-

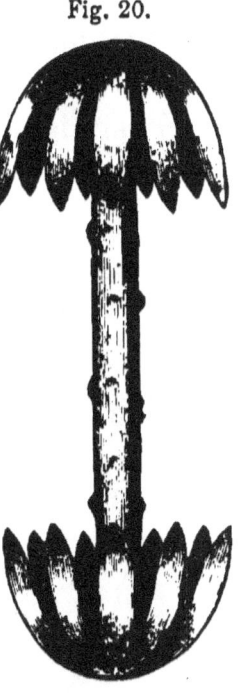

Fig. 20.

Mag. × 60.

quarters of an inch in thickness. Its colour is a deep buff, and when dried it greatly resembles the ordinary Turkey sponge, except that it is much finer. The spicules to be obtained from this species are very varying in their shapes, some being fashioned like the letters S and C, others are simple needles, nearly straight, and a few look like double anchors.

Fig. 21.

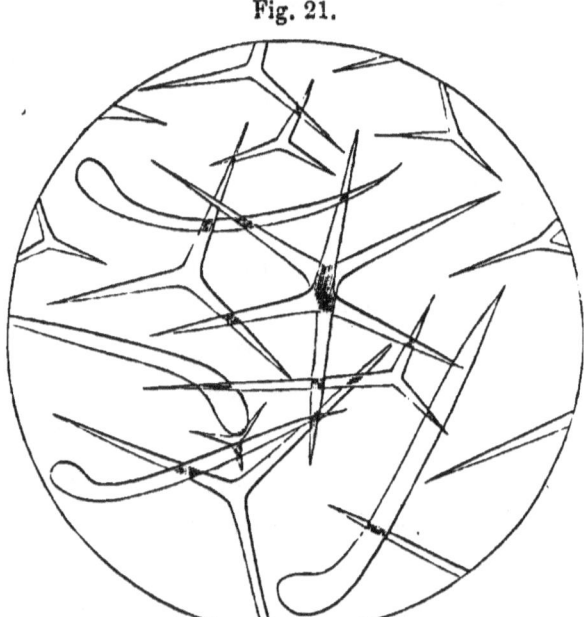

Spicules of *Grantia compressa*.

*Halina Bucklandi* is an inconspicuous and small specimen of these incrusting sponges. Its colour is a greyish-black, and its size a little over an inch across. You cannot well mistake it, not only on account of its colour, but also from its smooth and shiny appearance. *Leuconia nivea* is another unassuming object. Its colour, as expressed by its specific name, is a dirty white. The thickness of the sponge is only about a quarter of an inch, but its summits are raised to about three quarters of an inch, and rounded off. Its colour, and crisp and gritty feel, will at once serve to identify it. In the three-rayed form of its spicules, it appears to be related to the *Grantia*.

A more attractive object than those just mentioned is the *Hymeniacidon caruncula*, a red-lead, or orange-coloured sponge, about an inch in diameter, having ridges about a quarter of an inch high. Each of the little ridges or peaks is perforated as usual. There is very little appearance of "sponge-flesh" on this species, so that it may readily be distinguished from another belonging to the same genus, called *albescens*. The former has spicules pointed only at one end, whilst in the latter they are pointed at both ends. The latter is distributed over the rock in winding worm-like masses, of an orange-yellow or buff colour, and having a characteristic "spongy" feel. Moreover, it throws up a series of processes or filaments, some of which are an inch in length. The most abundant of all these rock-encrusting sponges, however, is *Microciona carnosa*. It is a well marked species, and one easily to be identified. Our readers will see the impossibility of our doing other than give verbal descriptions of these kinds of sponges, as none but coloured illustrations would otherwise give any idea of them. The colour of the species we are now dwelling upon is a pale Indian red. It occurs in thick, plump bands, about half an inch in width, which alternately swell and contract, meeting, uniting, and separating again, and thus creeping over and covering a considerable portion of rock. The apices on the surface have two or three openings, and the whole structure is thickly invested with granular flesh. The spicules in *Microciona* are of a very simple kind. Lastly, we may mention *Pachymatisma Johnstoni* as another of this British group, and one of the largest, sometimes obtaining the diameter of a foot. Its shape is of great service to the student, enabling him easily to recognise it. It is of a globose form, and a purplish-grey colour, having its smooth surface dotted with a few minute orifices. The whole flesh is of a dense yellow, in which are set simple and six-rayed spicules, the latter forming beautiful objects for the microscope.

Before proceeding to notice the British sponges of a larger and more decidedly "sponge-like" form and texture, which, however, are only to be obtained by dredging in deeper water, let us refer to one of the commonest objects to be met with at the seaside. You cannot fail to have noticed oyster and other thick shells bored and perforated in a very peculiar way, as in Figs. 22 and 23.

The outsides of oyster shells are often drilled by scores of these holes, and, as the section will show, these are continuous into a series of chambers. When examined fresh, and by the aid of a good pocket lens, you will see these holes coated and lined with a yellowish substance. Singularly enough, these perforations are the work of a sponge, called

Fig. 22.

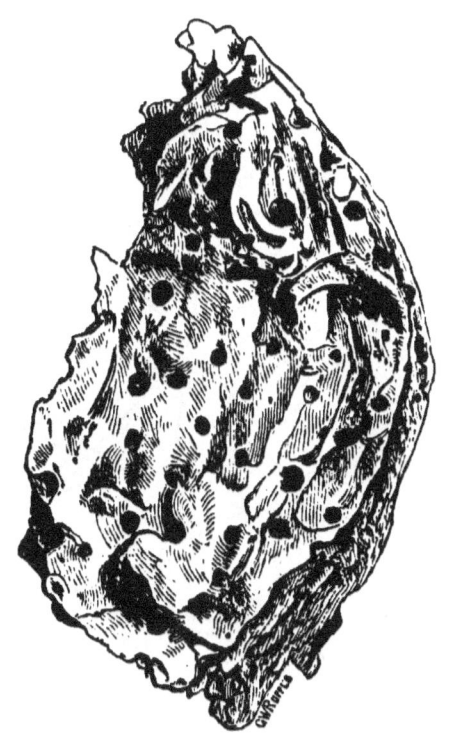

Portion of Oyster-shell perforated by *Clione*.

Fig. 23.

Section of Oyster-shell perforated by *Clione*.

*Clione*, of which the yellow substance is part. How it excavates the holes and cavities is a mystery, but it seems to have the power of dissolving away the lime for the purpose of living on the animal matter contained within the shell, just as a dog will crunch bones for the sake of their organic matter. That it is a true sponge, however, you may discover for yourself, if you will be at the trouble of boiling the yellow-looking substance in dilute nitric acid, as the result will furnish you with an abundance of pin-

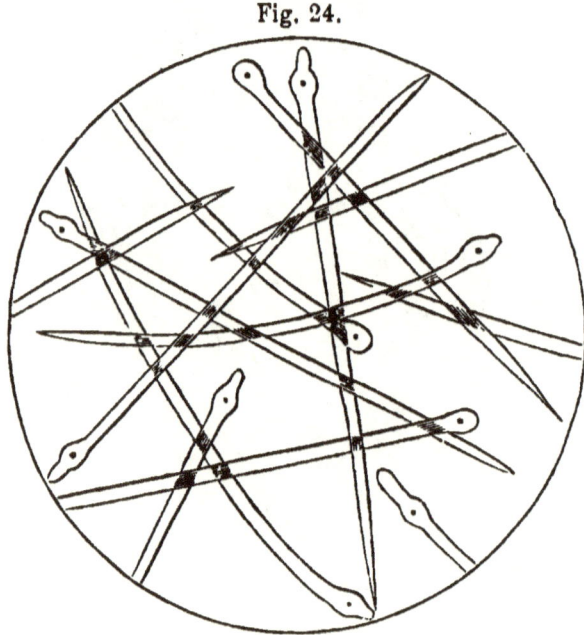

Fig. 24.

Spicules of sponge (*Clione celata*), magnified.

shaped spicules, like those shown in Fig. 24. Boring sponges must have been in existence for a long time, as we find the thick limy ossicles of *Belemnites*, fossilised in the chalk, perforated in a similar manner. The thick shells of the Tertiary strata indicate that the genus has been continuously in existence since then.

And now a word or two respecting our deeper water British sponges. We know nothing, in our northern temperate seas, of the large and luxuriant growth of sponges characteristic of warmer seas, of which the great "Neptune's Cup" may be taken as an example. The commonest and largest of our native sponges is *Chalina oculata* (Fig. 25), a branching and tree-shaped sponge, often found thrown up on the sands after a storm, which averages about nine inches in length. It is very variously branched, occasionally palmate or digitate, with the

Fig. 25.
*Chalina oculata*,
nat. size.

branches rounded or compressed and the surface even. As before observed, the *oscula* are arranged in lines, more or less on one side each branch. The margins of these orifices are slightly elevated, but scarcely noticeable. In the outer membrane may be found a few slender, needle-like spicules, but those of the interior, or skeleton, are shorter and stouter, and

Fig. 26.

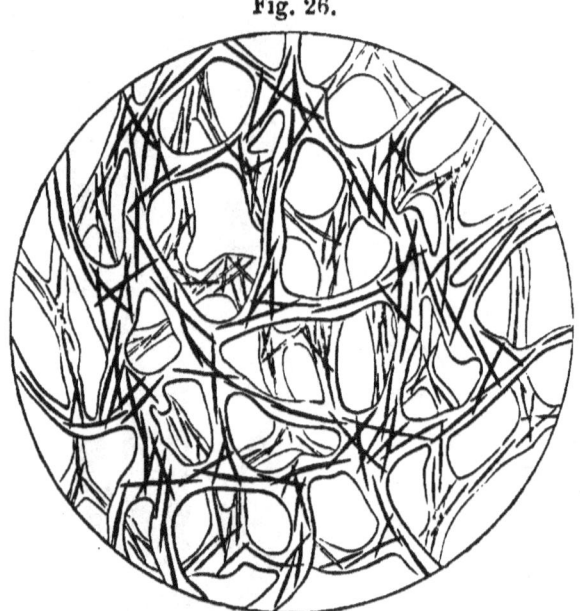

Section of *Chalina oculata*.

rather spindle-shaped. When this sponge is living, it is of a yellowish colour, with just a tinge of green. It changes rapidly after being uprooted, and passes into the usual colour of common sponge when dried. Fig. 26 will give our readers a good notion of the appearance of a portion of a section of this sponge under the microscope. There they will see the spicules mixed up with and strengthening the horny skeleton. Our readers must remember that the storm-cast specimens are nearly always denuded of the external membrane. In Fig. 27 is given an enlarged illustration of the spicules of this species. Another of our deeper water sponges, not as common, however, as that we have just been endeavour-

Fig. 27.

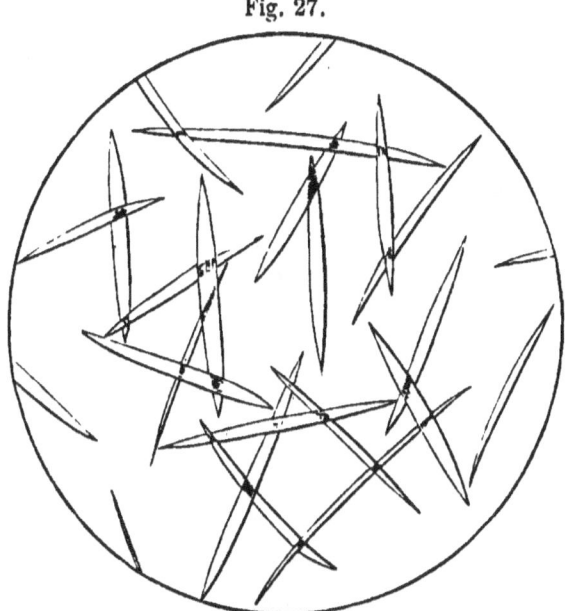

Spicules of *Chalina oculata*.

ing to describe, is the *Halichondria ramosa* (Fig. 28). It is smaller, firmer, and more compact than the *Chalina*, although there seems to be little difference else, except in this, that in *Chalina* there is a fibrous skeleton of keratose, whilst in *Halichondria* the spicules are interwoven together into a network. When alive, the latter is yellow, orange, flesh-colour, pink, or crimson, and is therefore a very beautiful object. It only acquires a brownish colour, as all the sponges seem to do, when in the dry state. In height this species is seldom more than three inches. Its appearance is often very variable, on account of the great difference in its ramification, the branches being frequently much compressed. As might be expected, considering what we know of the warmer waters of the Devonshire coasts, all the British sponges there met with are larger than usual. Thus, in the neighbourhood of Torquay specimens of the *ramosa* have been dredged as much as ten inches in height. When dried, this sponge presents a very marked difference from the *Chalina*, in that the spicules project all over the surface (see illustration) so as to give to it a hairy appearance. These spicules are much of a similar character, but differ in size from those of the *Chalina*, whilst there is an absence of them altogether in the membrane. In neither case are the spicules attractive as microscopic objects. Lastly, we would draw attention to a species which is quite as common as the *Chalina*

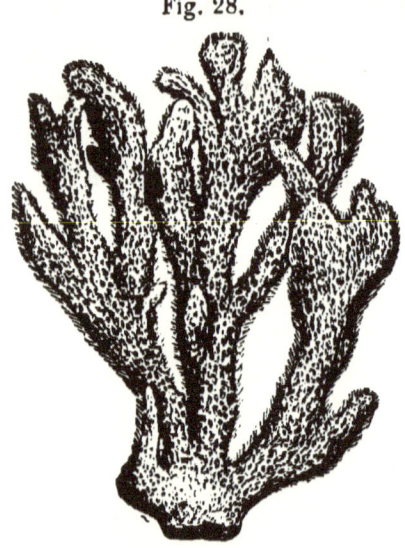

Fig. 28.

*Halichondria ramosa.*

*oculata*. This has been called the "crumb-of-bread" sponge (*Halichondria panicea*, Fig. 29), from its resemblance, when dried, to a piece of the crumb of white bread. When alive, however, its colour ranges from light ash to yellow, orange, or green. Its external shape varies exceedingly. Sometimes we find it enveloping the stems of larger seaweeds or zoophytes, or encrusting rocks or stones, as in Fig. 29, where it has done so in company with some sertularians. Its surface is quite smooth when the sponge is alive, but when dry it is minutely reticulated. For some time after it is dead, if the sponge masses are broken, it will be seen to be of a yellowish-green internally. The membrane of this species is exceedingly rich in spicules, and the entire skeleton is made up of spicules cemented together, as indeed is the rule with the other species of this order. These spicules are long and spindle-shaped, besides being a little curved (see Fig. 30). They are pointed at each end. When sections of all these sponges are mounted for the microscope, from the

Fig. 29.

*Halichondria panicea.*

surface inwards, a good deal more may be learned of their structure than if simple spicules alone were used.

Of course all our British species are too small to have any economic value. But they are well worthy of study, and will throw much light on the history of the lower forms of life. Sponges have served a

Fig. 30.

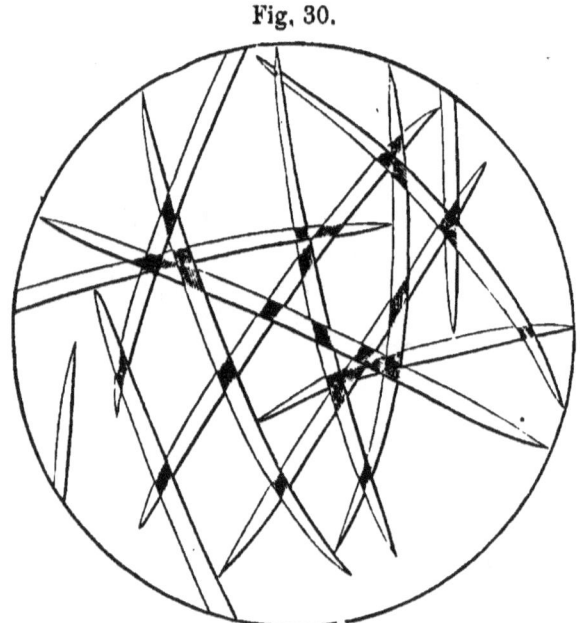

Spicules of *Halichondria panicea*.

wonderful part in the scheme of creation. By the decomposition of their protoplasm, or sarcode, chemical changes have been naturally promoted which have had very important results. The silicates of soda held in solution by sea-water have been precipitated by such chemical action, and the result has been the formation of bands and nodules of *flint*, such as we may see intersecting and alternating in any old chalk quarry. The spongeous origin of the greater part of such flints is now regarded as more or less settled. You can hardly chip off a thin flake, but you find it crowded with spicules, and with the internal casts of the same species of foraminifera as are to be found in the pure chalk. Flint seems to be forming in this manner now, especially in the deeper parts of the sea. The casts of recent foraminifera and corals have been repeatedly dredged up, to show that the process which subserved such a wonderful end in the cretaceous period, as well as when the chert beds of the older limestones were formed, is still silently going on. Surely we may say of these sponges, as Montgomery, in his "Pelican Island," did of the coral.

> "Slime their material, but the slime was turned
> To adamant by their petrific touch;
> Frail were their frames, ephemeral their lives—
> Their masonry imperishable. All
> Life's needful functions, food, exertion, rest,
> By nice economy of Providence,
> Were overruled to carry on the work
> Which out of water brought forth solid rock."

## V.

### HALF AN HOUR WITH SEA-WORMS.

WITH the exception of one or two notable instances, we can hardly say we are in this case inviting our readers to the study of a class of the most attractive objects. But the naturalist, more than anybody else, soon learns that "beauty is only in the eye of the beholder!" Objects which are interesting soon have an attraction of their own which is quite equivalent to mere beauty. Indeed, the study of natural history would be beneficial if it did no more than check that gross egotism of the human mind which unhesitatingly asks of any object it does not understand—"What is it good for?" without stopping to put the same question to itself. It teaches man rightly to understand his own place in the universe as a man—apart from his relation to higher laws as an intellectual and moral being. Geology shows that there is hardly a class of creatures now in existence that in its turn has not occupied the chief place in creation; so that, in this respect, man is only passing through the same grade.

The very name of "worms" has something traditionally repulsive about it. We have unfortunately, in our ignorance, learned to regard the creatures composing it as types of something degraded. This false idea has obtained too firm a hold on the popular mind to be shaken off at a moment. Zoology, however, considers no form imperfect. In the grand scheme of adaptation which characterises both the animal and vegetable kingdoms, it fails to see a single object that is not better suited to the habitat it lives in than it could be to any other. Hence if a "worm" be adapted to the circumstances of its life—if the latter have a distinct reference to its organs and structure, it is to all intents and purposes a *perfect* animal. People are so apt to confound *specialisation* of function with physiological perfection. Nothing of the kind. Being merely highly organised does not argue that the animal in which these organs exist is more perfect. Pope's remarkable line in this respect is zoologically and physiologically true:—

"As full, as perfect, in a hair as heart."

A more accurate knowledge of the habits and structure of the very creatures which have furnished the idea of degraded imperfection—the common earthworm—shows us that the Creator has as beneficently adapted this lowly organised object to the circumstances of its life as He has animals of a higher grade. Its very habit of "eating dust," which superstition has more or less connected with the "primal curse," is done for the purpose of extracting the animal matter richly diffused through the soil thus swallowed. The sea-worms, many of them, follow the same habit, as you may notice for yourself in the castings so abundantly sprinkling the finer portion of the sands at low water. Nay, this very habit was also indulged in millions of years ago, for we find in the oldest rocks in Great Britain, the *Cambrian*, strata ripple-marked and otherwise evidencing their shallow-water origin, which are thickly strewn over with the fossil castings of *Arencolites*.

Sea-worms are separated by naturalists into two great groups, *Tubicola* and *Errantia*. The former, as the name implies, inhabit tubes, some of which, as in the case of the *Serpulæ*, are formed of carbonate of lime, which is a genuine secretion from the body. Others exude a gummy substance, to which grains of sand and fragments of shells adhere, and strengthen it. The only healthy movement possessed by these creatures is that of moving a little up and down their tubes. Our readers cannot fail to have been struck with the marvellous abundance of one of these genera of sea-worms, the *Serpula*, Fig. 31. You may see them thickly clustering, in every degree of curve and coil, over the backs of oyster-shells, or the surfaces of stones which lie close to the low water mark. Well does this common species deserve the name given it of *Serpula contortuplicala*. But to see it in its beauty is a difficult task, and only to be fully enjoyed when

Fig. 31.
Sea-worm.

the creature has been placed in a marine aquarium for some time, and got more or less used to the place. Occasionally you may catch a glance at it spreading out its brilliant scarlet plumes, but the moment your shadow has fallen over the water, so sensitive is it, the plumes are withdrawn, and the tube closed by a scarlet-coloured plug, which when drawn down serves as the stopper. These plumes are the *branchiæ*—the organs of breathing. Every filament that gives to them their feather-like and graceful appearance is finely and abundantly ciliated. The surrounding water is disturbed by their waving movement, and thus not only furnishes them with fresh oxygen, but also brings to them their food. The blood thus aërated is then driven back to what serves as the heart by the contractile power of the branchiæ. As a rule, the sea-worms which do not possess tubes have the gills or branchiæ arranged in tufts along each side of the body, as in the lob-worm. But as the formation of a tube for defensive purposes forbids this arrangement in the serpula, we can at once see the beautiful arrangement which collects and places them at the head of the animal. The plug to which reference has just been made is nothing more than one of these branchial filaments modified and thickened. The movement up and down the tube is achieved by means of bristle-like attachments arranged along the sides. The rapidity with which the serpula can withdraw itself within its tube is strikingly in contrast with the slowness and caution it exhibits before it again exposes its beautiful plumes. The lower ends of these tubes are usually cemented to stones or shells, for the sake of attachment. Most of these tubed sea-worms creep out of their singular dwellings just before they die, or when they are very sickly, and this fact is useful to those who keep aquaria, as a signal for their removal, and before they can taint the water. We have two species of serpula peculiar to our coasts, that just mentioned and a rarer species, *Serpula triguetra*. The latter sometimes runs to a great length over the rocks and stones, and is not a very pleasant object for the hand to come in contact with, on account of the sharp, prickly ridges which distinguish it from its fellow.

These tubed worms have a great geological antiquity. We find them fossilised in the Silurian limestones, and in every formation since. In the chalk there occurs a species of serpula (*plicata*) which is found in contorted masses, running over the naked surface of shells, sea-urchins, &c., just as we find its modern representative thickly clustered on oysters. It thus becomes useful as a sort of chronometrical guide to the rate at which the chalk accumulated over the old sea bottoms. For instance, we know that when the fossil sea-urchins were alive they were covered with spines, so that it would have been impossible for the sea-worms to have then formed their tubes over them. But when the former died, the spines peeled off with the decomposing membrane, and left the surface naked. In this condition, amid the oozy mud, the serpulæ were glad to find a place where they could attach themselves, and in finding it on these shells, &c., they plainly tell us the chalk did not accumulate fast enough to bury them whilst they were living. The interior as well as the exterior of fossil shells is frequently found overrun by serpulæ, showing how the former had died, and the ligament which held the valves together been decomposed, before the mud collected over them. Two very common, but exceedingly minute tubed-worms, allied to the serpulæ, are the *Spirorbis communis* and *nautiloides* (Figs. 32 and 33).

Fig. 32.          Fig. 33.

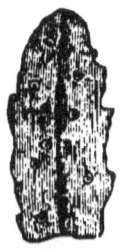 

*Spirorbis nautiloides* on *Fucus serratus*, nat. size.     *Spirorbis nautiloides*, × 25.

They are usually found adhering to the backs of the common sea-wrack, in many cases almost covering the fronds with their little coiled shells. The worms inhabiting these abodes closely resemble the serpula. They possess six branchial filaments, of a rose-pink tint, and the peduncle or plug, which look strikingly like angels' trumpets. A species nearly allied to these is abundant, in the fossil state, in the

Coal Measures, where it is seen attached to old fossil tree trunks, &c. Many people mistake the long white tubes, which may be seen ramifying through pieces of old wreck that have been cast ashore, for sea-worms. This, however, is a mistake, although the popular name of "ship-worms" (*Teredo navalis*) is always given to them. They are in reality a species of bivalve mollusc, which bore into and take up their lodgment in the wood, leaving the excavations lined with carbonate of lime for the sea-water to communicate with them and bring them their food.

Those of our readers who have visited the Crystal Palace Aquarium—a capital place for a young naturalist—will have noticed in one of the tanks a group of large-tubed sea-worms, with large feathery branchiæ. These are the *Sabella*, of which we have three or four species living in the deeper rock-pools along our coasts. Like the serpula, they are usually found in clusters, but not always so, and never so numerous as the former. They differ from them also in two or three very important particulars. First, they do not possess the operculum or plug, which is such a a marked feature in the living serpula. Second, their tubes are not composed of carbonate of lime. Instead of this, they secrete a kind of mucus, and this hardens, after having been strengthened by the adherence of grains of sand, &c. These tubes not unfrequently extend to several feet in length. The animals inhabiting them do not exhibit the delicate sensibility we have noticed as peculiar to the serpula. Occasionally they burrow in the sand, for the purpose of inserting their tubes. Others seem to prefer absolute freedom. The exquisite form and graceful motions of the gills or branchiæ of the Sabella have long been favourite topics for naturalists to descant upon. The *Terebella* is another sea-worm allied to the latter in many respects. It puts one in mind of the little caddis-worms to be met with in our ponds and ditches, more than anything else. You can hardly fail to meet with it if you turn over a heap of seaweeds lying between tides. The tubes are about the thickness of an ordinary tobacco-pipe, and are composed of sand, fragments of shells, &c., agglutinated together into a flexible tube. The mouth of the tube is fringed with a number of smaller hair-like tubes of a similar construction (Fig. 34). This worm is remarkable on account of the transformations through which its young pass. They appear first as embryos, furnished with cilia for swimming, and possessing a mouth and anus and alimentary canal. By-and-by the embryo gradually lengthens, the cilia become confined to a band behind the head and another near the tail. New segments are added one after the other, the tubercles and setæ developing in the same order, until at length a free-swimming Annelide ensues. This remarkable development of the egg of one animal to pass through the exact stage of another, is frequently repeated in the lower forms of life. After the *Terebella* has reached this stage it seems to repose. The cilia of the head are lost, and it gradually passes into the form such as we have described it, exuding a mucus and forming a tube.

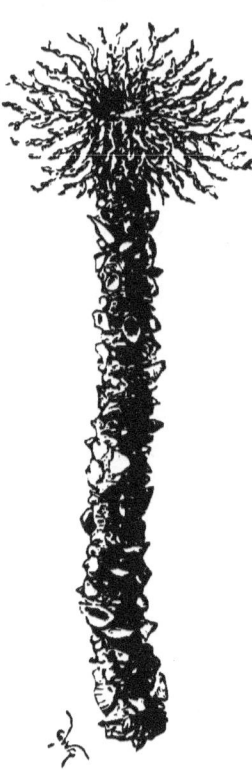

Fig. 34.

Tube of Terebella.

So far we have been dealing with objects which are not repulsive, but rather the contrary. It is possible, however, that the next group of sea-worms, the *Errantia*, may not be regarded with the same favour. In truth, many of them do not seem very pleasant objects to handle. But they are well worth half an hour's study, and our observant readers are sure to meet with some of them during their recreative zoologising by the seashore. We will take the little "lob-worm" first (*Arenicola piscatorum*), so called on account of its being a favourite bait for shore fishing. The antiquity of this humble and obscure object is second to that of no other creature, for we find the "castings" of extinct species (*Arencolites*) in the oldest stratified rocks of Great Britain. The modern species has a rapid burrowing power, retreating out of sight in an instant. It excavates a series of chambers in the sands, literally eating its way along, and passing the excreted sands out; after the organic matter with which they were charged has been extracted in its passage through the worm's body. When you examine it carefully you perceive that it has no eyes or jaws, as some of the "errant" sea-worms have. It breathes by means of thirteen pairs of branchiæ, which are arranged on each side. The digestive system of the *true* "Errantia," of which we may take the common Nereis as an example, is very peculiar. They possess a mouth, horny jaws, gullet, stomach, intestines, and anus, so that it will be perceived they are not by far such lowly organised creatures as might at first be supposed. Indeed, the worms as a class (*Anarthropoda*) stand relatively higher than the anemones, sea-urchins, &c., on account of their more complex specialization. In this respect, therefore, the rule laid down by Von Baer holds good, that "the progress of development is from the general to the special." The circulating apparatus in these worms consists of a system of vessels with contractile walls, the vessels being filled sometimes with red, and at others with a greenish fluid. This is termed in scientific language the "pseudo-hæmal system." Respiration is carried on either by the general surface of the body or by means of gills or branchiæ set apart for the purpose. The nervous system is gangliated, and well developed. Although most of them are furnished with what look very much like antennæ, a little observation will detect that these are not jointed, as they are in insects and crustaceans. The sexes are sometimes distinct, and at others united in the same individual. This arrangement, however, is exceedingly variable, for what is called "gemmation"—that is, the budding of new individuals—is also carried on as a means of increasing the species. Singularly enough, there is a kind of "alternation of generation" exemplified here, similar to that so well known in the natural history of the plant-lice (*aphides*). For instance, a worm that has been produced by "gemmation" will often produce young that will lay eggs; whilst the individuals resulting from the latter can only bring forth "buds" or "gemmules."

The *Nereis margaritacea*, or "Sea-centipede," is a sea-worm that well deserves its specific name of "pearly," as every one will confess who has seen its changeable metallic lustre, and its opalescent tints beneath. Generally, it ranges from brown to dark green in the colour of its upper side, subject to the lustrous variations above mentioned. This worm is one of the finest and commonest of the species which haunt our shores. Through the light brown of the back you can see the blood-vessel, or "dorsal heart," contracting at intervals of a few seconds, and then dilating. It is not at all uncommon for this species to take up its head-quarters in an empty univalve, which it sometimes shares in company with the Hermit Crab. Its two eyes and proboscis are plainly visible, and its foot-tubercles and bristles (*setæ*) enable it to crawl along with some rapidity, and to swim with even greater ease. The gills are arranged in tufts on the back and sides. Distantly allied to this species is the *Eunice gigantea*, whose greater length and different colour enable you at once to distinguish it. Very often the latter species numbers over four hundred segments, and is four feet long. Its gills are well developed and large, and its mouth is armed with seven or eight rather formidable horny jaws. *Polynoe* is another kind of sea-worm, which you may find by turning over any flat stone between the tide ranges. It is about an inch and a half in length, of a brown colour, and is rather an insignificant looking object. When you examine it more carefully, you perceive that its back is covered with a series of very thin plates which overlap each other. Far more attractive creatures are the two species of *Phyllodoce*, so called on account of the "leaf-shaped" organs on their backs, by means of which they swim. One of these, *Phyllodoce viridis*, is, as its name signifies, of a bright grass-green colour. Seek out a place near low water where the young mussels are attached to the rocks in great numbers, and you will hardly fail to see this pretty worm, which can scarcely be distinguished sometimes from a thin strip of seaweed. Its length is only about three inches; but in the other species, *P. laminosa*, it frequently extends to a foot, and includes two or three hundred segments. The latter is even more striking, when carefully observed, than the former. The rainbow colours which seem to chase each other as it throws itself into the most graceful curves, in order to adjust itself to the inequalities of the rock, and the pearly flesh-colour of the under parts, render it really a charming object. If you disturb it gently you will notice a remarkable change come over it. The under side of its head rises from the ground, swells, and then seems to turn itself inside out. Presently a great pear-shaped bag is protruded, eight times as long and three as broad as the entire head. The surface of this new organ is rough, and small rows of tubercles may be seen clustering round the extremity. This peculiar apparatus is called the "proboscis," and is supposed to be used for the capture of its prey. Finally, we must notice another sea-worm, by far the most repulsive and ugly of the whole class. This is the *Nemertes*. It appears like a long, thin, black cord, entwined round any object it can get, and so far greatly resembling a miniature serpent. This likeness is further carried out in its head, which is remarkably snake-like. It is a deadly foe to the tubed-worms, such as the serpula and sabella, which it literally drags out of their retreats to devour.

Lastly, let us briefly draw attention to a common species of sea-worm which constitutes a group by itself. This is the *Sipunculus*, a creature remarkable for its appearing to connect the "sea-cucumbers" with the Annelida. In shape it is not at all unlike an ordinary garden cucumber, with the stalk attached. This stalk-like portion is protruded and withdrawn at the animal's pleasure, the tip expanding and throwing out a series of white thread-like tentacles. One species inhabits deserted univalves, like the Nereis, and seems especially partial to that of the periwinkle. It has a trick, when properly housed, of cementing a wall of sand across the mouth of the shell, leaving a small orifice through which it can protrude its curious trunk and obtain its food. In all these variations in animal structure, the devout mind cannot fail to trace the perfect accordance maintained between them and the equally striking variations in the physical circumstances of their habitats. This harmony, like a silver thread, runs through and connects the entire range of the animal kingdom.

## VI.

HALF AN HOUR WITH CORALLINES.

It will not be possible for the sea-side visitor who has troubled himself to look for the objects already mentioned, to pass over a number of objects which go by the common name of *Corallines*. Occasionally, also, they are known by the more fanciful one of "sea-firs," on account of their resemblance to a miniature pine. Popularly, they are regarded as a kind of seaweed; but the young zoologist will not be long ere he find that they are *colonies* of animals, and that there is connected with their life-history one of the most curious and wonderful changes to be met with in the whole animal kingdom. The objects themselves are common enough, and are to be found in every rock-pool, or clinging to the fronds and stems of the larger seaweeds, or attached to the upper surfaces of such large shells as the oyster. When cast ashore after a storm, they are mostly dead, although it is always worth your while to try them in your bell-glass, unless you perceive they are old and withered specimens. Examine them with a common magnifying glass, and you will see they are composed of a *horny* stem, usually jointed and hollow, the hollows communicating with every part, and being, in fact, the means by which the polypites which dwell in the cups are connected with each other.

These compound animals belong to the class *Hydrozoa*, so named on account of their relationship to the little Hydras of our fresh-water ponds. It contains two orders, the members of both of which live in British seas, and therefore are to be sought for and found in beach rambles. The Hydrozoa are remarkable for their peculiar specialization, notwithstanding they appear such insignificant objects. Each of the little animals living in the cups planted at the joints or projections, is called a "zooid." These have assigned to them as their duty the providing of the food for the colony. They possess no reproductive powers whatever. In order to perpetuate the species, therefore, a peculiar set of buds are developed for this purpose. They are wholly unlike their brethren of the same colony, for when they are ripe and detached, they lead an entirely independent existence, resembling jelly-fish. The latter bring forth both ova and sperm-cells, and these fructify and settle down to the plant-like appearances of the "sea-firs" or corallines.

Commencing with the first of these two orders, the *Corynida*, we meet with the *Tubularians*, or "Pipe Corallines." These are never prolonged to form the little cups in which the polypites are contained, the horny substance stopping short at their bases. This is one of the distinguishing features between the "Pipe Corallines" and the "sea-firs," or *Sertularians*. The bases of the pipes are attached to shells or stones, the pipes themselves being composed of the horny material before mentioned. Each pipe is filled with a reddish fluidy flesh, or "cœno-

Fig. 35.

Oaten Pipe Coralline.

sarc," which gives exit at its mouth to a single polypite. These polypites are surrounded with tentacles, and are conical, almost resembling rosebuds. Their conical or "club-shaped" form gives the name of *Corynida* to them, the latter word being the Greek for a club. The mouth is situated at the apex of this club. The number of tentacles varies in the different species, and the generative buds, or young, are produced at their bases. One species, the "Oaten Pipe Coralline" (*Tubularia indivisa*, Fig. 35) is really a very beautiful object. It lives in about

Fig. 36.

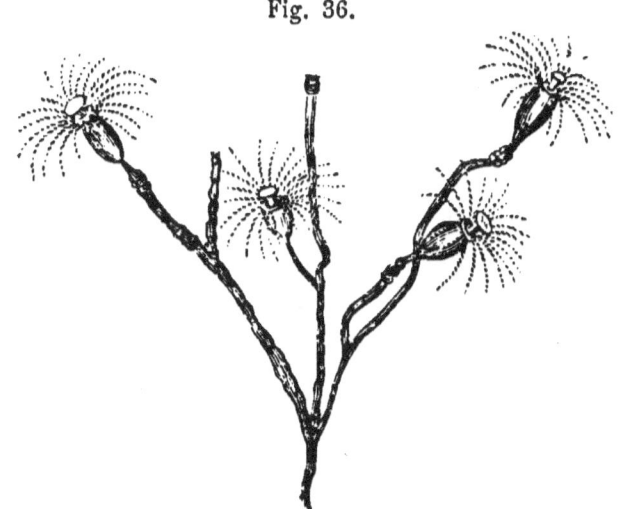

Branched Pipe Coralline, magnified.

thirty or forty feet of sea-water, and when its tentacles are expanded, it resembles a brilliant scarlet flower, or rather the pipes seem like so many small glasses, each containing a flower. This species can hardly be called "compound" in the sense in which other corallines are. There is one nearly allied to it, however, which is truly compound, the "Branched Pipe Coralline" (*Tubularia ramea*, Fig. 36). It is much smaller than its predecessor, but is an exquisitely beautiful object, the brown horny tubes terminating in what seem bright yellow and red flowers.

The *Sertularians* are much commoner than the species just mentioned, about twenty species occurring in British seas, besides those of allied genera. The horny envelope, which is all that is left after these objects have been cast ashore and dried, is called the "polypary." Its duty is to enclose the common flesh of the colony ("cœnosarc"), whilst it is prolonged to form a number of little cups, called "hydrotheca." In these live the animals proper, under the name of "polypites." They are soft and retractile, and are provided with delicate tentacles, capable of seizing and appropriating their prey. The nutriment thus obtained by each polypite serves more or less to support the entire organism. In some respects they resemble the Tubularians, in requiring special generative buds for the purposes of reproduction. The Sertularians are divided into five genera, of which only *Thuiaria* has the living animal or polypite imbedded in the axis. Another has the cups confined to one side of the axis (*Hydrallmannia*, or *Plumularia*); the remaining three having two rows of cups or cells arranged on each side the stem and branches. The student will find no small degree of inconvenience in his earlier attempts to thoroughly comprehend the names of these common objects, on account of the confusion which exists, by reason of different zoologists having given different names to the same species. Let us commence with one of these Sertularians, the "Bottle-brush Coralline" (*Thuiaria thuia*, Fig. 37). As is shown in the woodcut, this species is usually found attached to shells in tolerably deep water. The cells or calycles are imbedded in the substance of the branches, as shown in Fig 38, the capsules being pear-shaped and smooth. A species nearly allied to it is the *T. articulata*, known by its more feathery appearance.

Fig. 37.

*Thuiaria thuia*, natural size.

The "Sickle Coralline" (*Hydrallmannia falcata*, Fig. 39) is so called on account of the appearance presented by the arrangement of the cells on one side of the curved branches only. This genus formerly went by the name of *Plumularia*, under which the student will find it in the older works on hydrozoa. It is a very common, but exceedingly elegant species, about six inches in height, having slender branches which twist about in a *spiral* manner. The cells containing the polypites are arranged along those branches. It is usually found adhering to rocks and shells by means of little wrinkled tubes, from which it rises into erect stems. These are surrounded from bottom to top with pinnated branches, the smaller of which have little cells on the side and bend inwards. A magnified

Fig. 38.  Fig. 39.

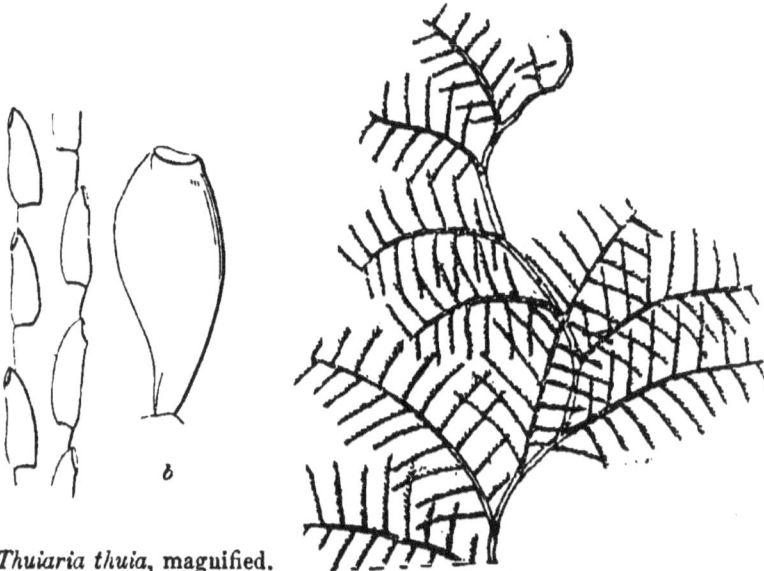

*Thuiaria thuia*, magnified.
b. capsule.

Sickle Coralline.

view of these side cells is given in Fig. 40, where the reader will see their crowded arrangement. The capsules seen in Fig. 41 are pear-shaped, slightly ribbed when dry, and having a contracted tubular mouth. These are most abundant in the spring.

*Sertularia abietina* is a coralline even more abundant than the last-named. It is this species which the reader must have noticed growing in little groves on the surfaces of old oyster shells, and its specific

HALF AN HOUR WITH CORALLINES. 91

name is well given to it, for it does not require any effort of the imagination to see in it the likeness of a fir tree. Hence it is named the "sea-fir" *par parenthèse*, and this has been extended to all the Sertularians, whence their popular generic name. It has a slightly waving stem (Fig. 42), with branches on each side. Its height is usually seven or eight

Fig. 40.

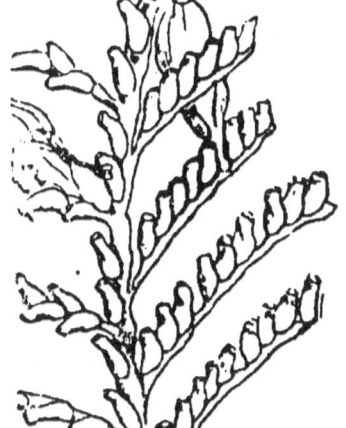

Fig. 41.

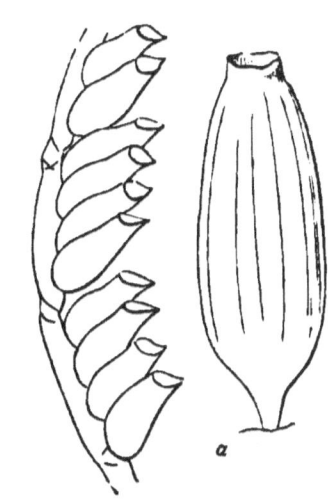

Sickle Coralline, magnified.

*Hydrallmannia falcata*, magnified.
a. capsule.

inches, sometimes more, and its breadth across the branches about three. The latter are usually shorter towards the apex. Both along each side of the stem and branches every available spot is occupied with cells, each enclosing a separate animal when alive. These cells, or calycles, are large and flask-shaped (Fig 43), having their mouths turned outwards and upwards. The capsules are ovate, with a short mouth, and smooth or slightly wrinkled across when dry. The "Lily Coralline" (*Sertularia rosacea*, Fig. 44) usually occurs as a parasite on other zoophytes. Recently this species has had transferred to it the generic name of *Diphasia*, and this genus includes six other species. The difference is based on the presence of a spherical pouch in the upper portion of the capsule, which is absent in the true sertularians. This species is the smallest, in size, of the group. Indeed, it is one of the most delicate of all this class of zoophytes, the shoots being

Fig. 42.

The Sea Fir.

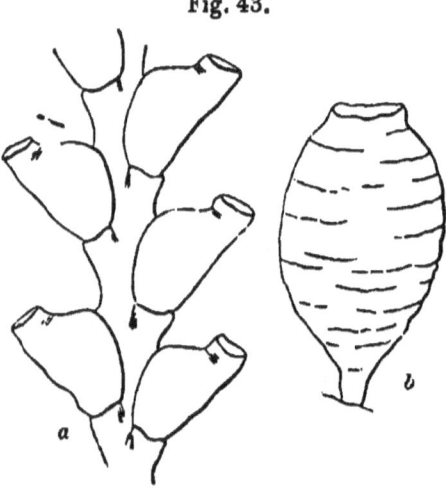

Fig. 43.

*Sertularia abietina*. a. calycles ; b. capsule, magnified.

exceedingly slender, and the texture thin. The capsules are liable to folding and wrinkling, when dry, on this account. The latter have eight longitudinal ridges, which terminate in as many projections of the apex (Fig. 45, *b c*). At the outside, *Diphasia rosacea* is never above two inches in height. And yet small and delicate though it be, it spreads rapid destruction around the place where

Fig. 44.

Lily Coralline.

it takes up its abode. Another species of *Diphasia*, irregularly branched, which may also be collected, is that known as the "Sea-Tamarisk (*D. tamarisca*). This, however, is of a strong, robust habit, and often grows to a large size. The cells have the upper half diverging, with a three-toothed aperture. The male capsules are the smallest. These are somewhat heart-shaped, and are generally arranged in rows. The female capsules are larger, and usually much lacerated at the mouth. It is not so common a species as the others, but, like them, lives in tolerably deep water, anchored to shells, &c. *D. attenuata* resembles the "Lily Coralline," but is of much firmer texture, so that the cells do not shrivel in drying. The capsules also have strong spines

Fig. 45.

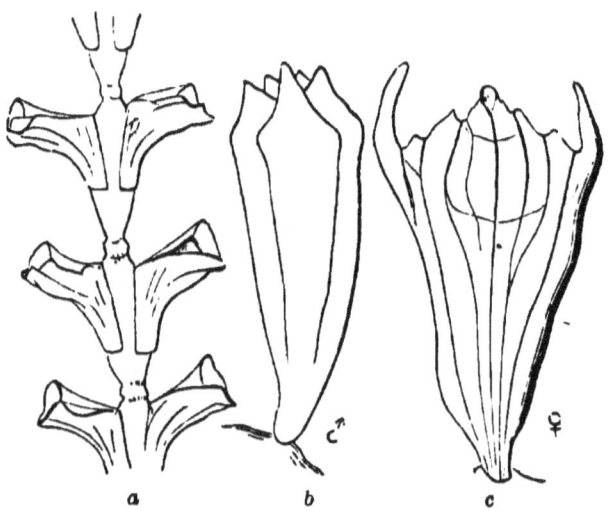

*Diphasia rosacea*, magnified. *a.* calycles; *b.* male capsule; *c.* female capsule.

at the apex, with six longitudinal ridges. Like the "Lily Coralline," it is usually parasitic on other zoophytes. *D. fallax* has a feathery appearance, and usually bears a number of curled tendrils. The stems are thick and dark coloured, the calycles, or cells, are tubular and diverging, and the capsules of an elongate shape, surmounted by four strong spines.

This species seems to be confined to the northern coasts of Britain, where it is parasitically attached to others. There are three other species of *Diphasia*, of which one, *alata*, is very rare. *D. pinnata* and *D. pinaster* are peculiar, the former being confined to the coasts of Devon and Cornwall, where it occurs in deep water. Its height is about six inches, and, when dry, its colour is dark. The cells or calycles are rather small, springing but little from the stem, and having a wide, even mouth (Fig. 46). The capsules are produced freely, the male being only one-third the size of the female, and bluntly toothed at their apex. The female capsules are egg-shaped, and divided by four longitudinal lines into four distinct lobes. *D. pinaster* includes what have been considered to be two distinct species. Its colour is a light brown, and it grows to a height of from two to six inches. The cells are cylindrical, the upper half being turned abruptly outwards. The male capsules are ovate, and almost four square in the upper portion, having a spine at each angle. On

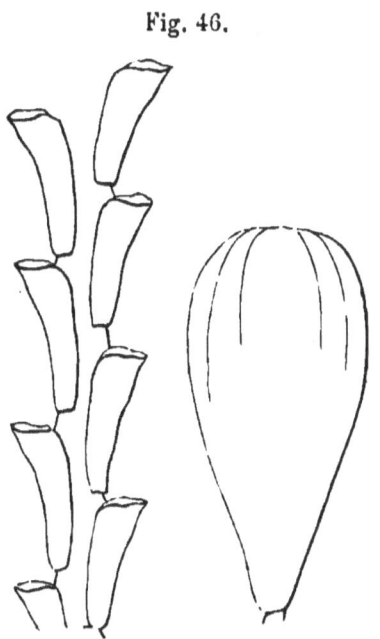

Fig. 46.

*Diphasia pinnata*, magnified.

the other hand, the male capsules are regularly oval, with four ridges running down them, and about eight spines running in two series on the upper part (Fig. 47). This species, however, unlike the others just described, is tolerably abundant, and seems to have a pretty general distribution.

The true sertularians have been grouped according to the arrangement of their cells, like the genus

Fig. 47.

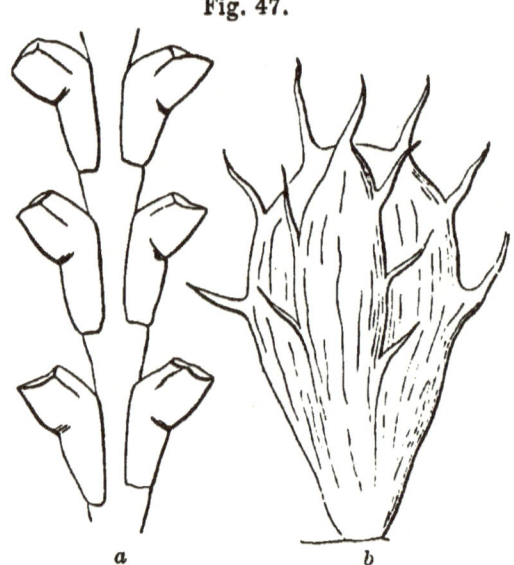

*Diphasia pinaster.* a. calycles; b. female capsule.

*Diphasia.* Two species are very small, and but slightly branched, one having its cells arranged in an opposite manner, with the branches regularly pinnate. This species, *Sertularia filicula*, is the only one in which this peculiarity occurs. Perhaps the commonest form, and that most likely and most abundantly to be met with by the collector, is the

"Sea-hair Coralline" (*S. operculata*, Fig. 48). It will be found usually attached to seaweeds, and growing to a height of from three to six inches. The time to look out for it is after a storm, when lumps as big as an orange are washed ashore. It takes its popular name from the circumstance of its

Fig. 48.

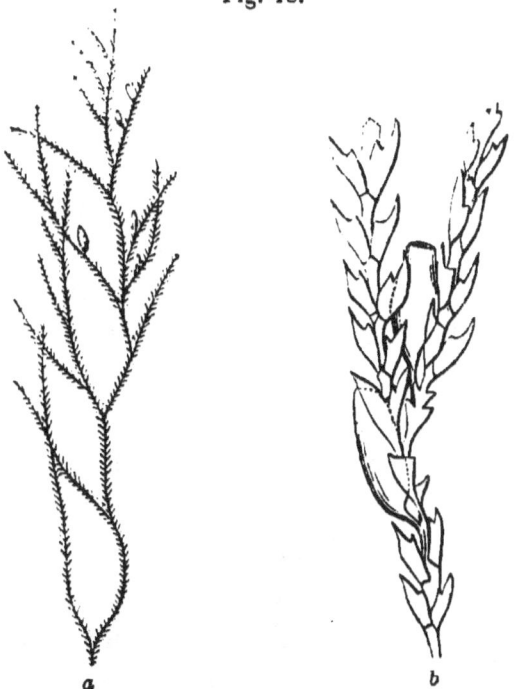

*Sertularia operculata.* a. natural size; b. magnified.

growing in tufts, like bunches of hair. Dr. Johnston, in his work on zoophytes, remarks that it was from the great resemblance of the cells to the capsules of mosses that the earlier botanists drew conclusions respecting the vegetable character of corallines; an idea not yet exploded, and which is more or less retained in the word "zoophyte," or animal-plant. In the species of which we are speaking, the cells or calycles end in a sharp point, with a small, intermediate tooth (see Fig. 48, *b*). The capsules are large and pear-shaped (Fig. 49), and have a circular hole. *S. operculata* lives a little below the low-water mark, and is parasitic.

Fig. 49.

Capsule of *Sertularia operculata*.

Every one must have seen the pretty little object which goes by the name of the "Sea-oak Coralline" (*Sertularia pumila*, Figs. 50, 51). It is of a greenish colour, and occurs in considerable abundance on the common serrated wrack. Indeed, the latter is often invested with such a quantity of it as almost to have its fronds weighed down with it. The illustration will easily convey an idea of how this little zoophyte clings to seaweeds, and also give a good notion of what it is like. The shoots are seldom more than half an inch in height, and are threadlike, and very sparingly branched. The *hydras* inhabiting the cells or calycles, when examined with a strong magnifying glass, are seen to possess fourteen to sixteen tentacles. When these are displayed the hydra usually extrudes its body far beyond the rim

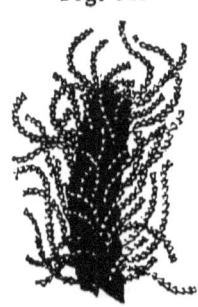

Fig. 50.

Sea-oak Coralline.

of the cell. It may be this particular species which Crabbe the poet had in view when he wrote—

"Involved in sea-wrack, here you find a race,
Which science, doubting, knows not where to place."

Since the poet saw it growing in abundance along the Suffolk shore, science has found out exactly where to place it, and the due zoological value attached to each function in the biological scale. The species of sertularia called *filicula* is known by the popular name of "Fern Coralline." As before remarked, it is the only one of the genus having feathery

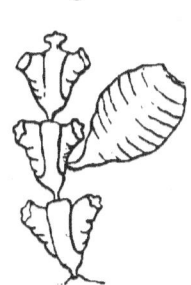

Fig. 51.

Sea-oak, magnified.

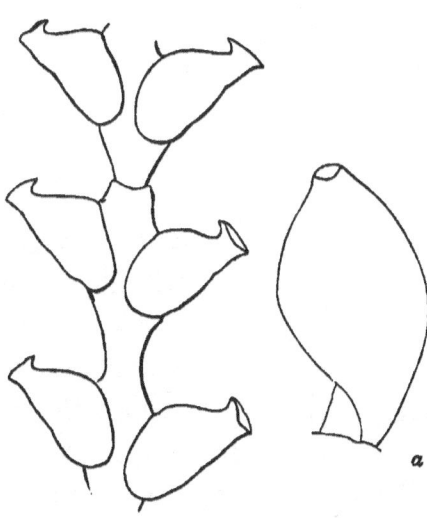

Fig. 52.

*Sertularia filicula*, magnified. *a*. capsule.

branches and oppositely arranged cells (Fig. 52).

It is more slender and delicate than the majority of the pinnate zoophytes, and is cast ashore in large tangled masses. It may easily be known by its zig-zag stems, and its peculiar colour and delicacy. As may be seen in the illustration, the calycles are flask-shaped, and the capsules pear-shaped, with a short tubular mouth. *Sertularia fusca* is rather a rare species, and is very small, with its calycles in two rows, and the mouths of the calycles turned in opposite directions. The "Squirrel's Tail Coralline" (*Sertularia argentea*, Fig. 53) is also small, but its branches are very rigid and erect. The calycles are short, and swollen below. It is the most common of all the species which occur on shells in deep water, and, after a storm, when the empty valves are cast on the beach, it may be found dead, but still adhering to them. The "Sea-cypress Coralline" (*Sertularia cupressina*, Fig. 54) has long wiry stems, with its branches drooping, and not as rigid as in the last mentioned species. Its calycles are longer, tubular, and with a two-lipped aperture,

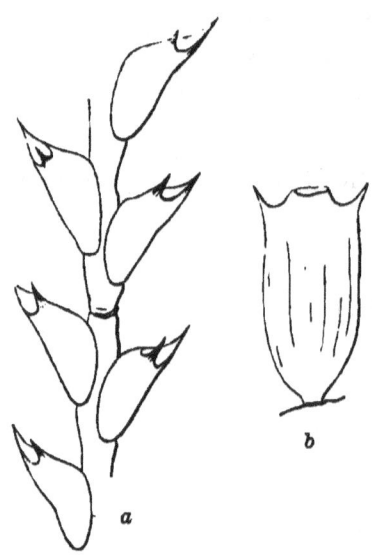

Fig. 53.

*Sertularia argentea.* a. calycles; b. capsule.

the capsules being similar in both species. In the latter they have two spines at the upper end, and a prominent mouth. Yet another species of "sea-fir" is *S. rugosa*, which is usually found parasitic on the fronds of the sea-mat, as well as on seaweeds.

There are many other kinds of zoophytes which the observing eyes of our readers may detect. Of these, perhaps the *Campanularidæ* are the prettiest, with their slender stalks terminating in crystal bells, so as to richly deserve the name they have borrowed from the well-known flower. In the species grouped under this division, the cells are stalked, a distinction between them and the sertularians, in which no such arrangement exists.

Fig. 54.

*Sertularia cupressina. a.* calycles ; *b.* capsule.

Their reproduction is by budding, the medusoid, glassy buds being free-swimming, and producing ova and germ cells, as in others of the hydrozoa. The *Campanularidæ* are very small, and usually parasitic on the fronds and stems of seaweeds, to which they cling like so many delicate hairs. Another peculiar zoophyte is the "Bird's-head Coralline" (*Cellularia avicularis*). It is a delicate, feathery object, greatly resembling some of the finer seaweeds, and is two or three inches high, growing like a miniature tree. When examined with a strong lens, the branches appear to be studded with cells, each furnished with a "bird's head" and "beak"-like process. The illusion is carried out by this beak continuing to open and shut, and the head keeping up a constant nodding to and fro, so that the result is quite comical. Nor should we omit drawing attention to another zoophyte, which the visitor will be pretty certain to find, the "Lobster's Horn Coralline" (*Antennularia antennina*). It derives its name from its strong likeness to the long jointed antennæ of the lobster. It is stiff and unbranched, and around each joint may be seen a whorl of delicate hairs, in the axils of which is seated the cell and glassy cup of a polypite.

We have already referred to the wonderful system of what may be regarded as allied to that known to naturalists by the name of "alternation of generation," which prevails among the hydrozoa. It is now known for a fact that these animals lead a most varied and active life. At one stage of their existence we find them skimming the sea as perfectly radiated animals, clothed in masses of translucent jelly, and even in many species giving out phosphorescent light. In others they throw out long tentacles, which sting the hand that dares to meddle with them. In fact, the connection of the medusæ with corallines appears quite incredible to the student when he first makes his acquaintance with it. Agassiz has described a large umbrella-shaped jelly-fish (*Cyanea arctica*), whose disk measured seven feet across, and whose tentacles were above fifty feet long, and yet this was produced from a little coralline not more than half an inch in height when full grown! Few, however, of the meduseans produced from the corallines reach this enormous size, but they make up for it by their countless myriads, which people every wave. Only

Fig. 55.

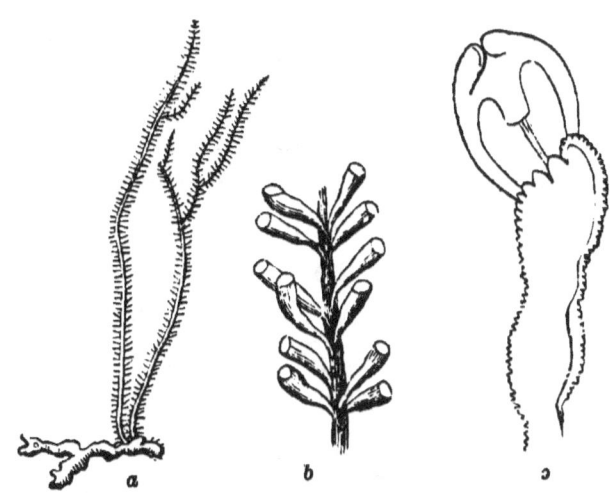

*a. Lafœa dumosa*, natural size. *b*. Polyp cells of the same, mag.
*c*. Young Sertularian Medusa, from *Lafœa*.

one species of *Sertularia* (*rugosa*) is known to produce meduseans, the usual method of reproduction in this group being already explained. This was called *Lafœa dumosa* (Fig. 55) by Lamouroux, and it was termed by Professor Edward Forbes the most active polyp he ever saw. When the generation buds, to which we alluded at the beginning of the present article, have become detached, they assume the form of true acalephæ, or jelly-fish. Here, then, we have a creature totally different from its immediate progenitor, the coralline! The medusoids are each furnished with a pedicel, which is in reality the mouth and stomach, and these hang down from the centre, as seen in Fig. 56. Round the edge of the umbrella-shaped disk may be seen hanging a series of fibrils, or "gemmæ." These, when detached, become separate animals. Besides them, the jelly-fish produces eggs, each of which is clothed with ciliæ, so as to be able to swim about. Eventually it becomes pear-shaped, and the narrowest end at length fixes itself to some stone or shell, and shoots up into an ordinary coralline, such as we have been endeavouring to describe. Our readers will agree that a more remarkable incident than this it is impossible to conceive. We are accustomed to the marvellous transformation by means of which an inconspicuous grub is changed to a gaudy butterfly; but this development of huge, transparent, free-swimming jelly-fish from objects so infinitely smaller, and even then harbouring colonies of such parents, is a wonder even more striking! However, such must necessarily be the influence of a better acquaintance with the Creator's works, resulting in an admiration compounded of awe and love, but deepening and widening as we see this wisdom reflected in the "works of His hands."

## VII.

### HALF AN HOUR WITH JELLY-FISH.

THERE are few sea-side visitors who are not acquainted with the unshapely and unsightly masses of jelly-looking substances occasionally strewn on the beach. Let the sea be unusually rough for a day or a night, and these objects will be met with more abundantly than sensitive eyes care to behold. When seen under these disadvantageous circumstances, however, it should be remembered that everything tells against them. It is not to be expected that creatures so loosely constructed as these jelly-fish actually are, should assume graceful and elegant shapes anywhere but in water, where their parts could present their natural appearances. Accordingly a person judging of jelly-fish by stranded specimens would be as far from forming an idea of their elegant outlines when alive in the sea, as if he had never seen such objects at all. Let him take a boat, and on a clear, sunny day, when the water is stiller than usual, amuse himself at a short distance from land, by gazing over its sides into the green depths below. Presently he may see one of our common jelly-fish come swimming by, its umbrella-like disk looking like a creature built of the most transparent glass, and its movements in the water, effected by its rythmical contractions and expansions, of the most graceful character, catching the light here and there on its surface, and reflecting it to the eye in iridiscent flashes. Once seen in their native element, jelly-fish cannot fail to be appreciated ever afterwards.

The natural history of these animals is perhaps more interesting than that of any other group so lowly organised. We have already referred to the connection of some species of jelly-fish with the corallines, and endeavoured to show that many of them are nothing more than the free-swimming buds of the latter. One species after another of jelly-fish, as their habits and origin have thus been more closely studied, has accordingly been withdrawn from the position in which it had been placed, and classed as the young of corallines. The whole of the sub-class *Discophora*, or *Medusidæ*, is regarded as questionable on this account; for, if there exist some of its members which at present appear to be medusæ, a further study may possibly relegate them to the same place as their brethren. From this our readers will get some idea of the muddle into which the technical study of these animals has been thrown, and it is not possible to get two text-books of zoology which give the same information concerning them.

One of the commonest of our jelly-fishes, to be found in most of our British harbours and at the mouths of our tidal rivers, is the crimson-ringed jelly-fish (*Aurelia aurita*). Not only is it a familiar object, but its beauty is equal to any of its congeners. It averages from six to eight inches in diameter, but is often larger, especially off the southern coasts. Its common name is given to it on account of the four crimson-coloured rings which may be seen relieving the otherwise glassy body. This species swims by the regular contraction and expansion of the body, and is therefore placed among the *pulmonigrade* jelly-fish, on account of the pulsations which propel it through the water resembling those of the lungs. The crimson rings mentioned are reproductive organs. Generally speaking, most of the bell-shaped or umbrella-shaped jelly-fish have peculiar organs hanging down their interior, much as a bell clapper hangs from the inside of a bell. These are called the *polypite*, and their functions are digestive, or alimentary. In the case of the species we are mentioning, a kind of pouch may be seen terminating the margins of the polypite, and it is now known that this is for ova. When the young are extruded they swim away as minute, flat, jelly-like bodies, aided by cilia, the usual method of progression with the ova of animalculæ and other creatures, and even, as we saw in the " seaweeds," with the spores of those plants.

Let us follow these little ova after their extrusion. The first thing noticeable is their shape, which is so flat, that when in this stage they were regarded as a distinct species, and went by the name of *Planula*.

The change which ensues transforms these flat-looking objects into a pear-shape. It now settles down to a sedentary existence, attaching itself to some submarine rock, and hanging downwards. A depression gradually forms, and tentacles begin to be protruded. In this stage it is the well-known *Hydra tuba*—an animal common in marine aquaria. Its height, however, is only about one-sixth of an inch. What is most singular is that it not unfrequently lives even for years in this condition, without showing signs of a change. Eventually we find the body enlarging in thickness and length, and we see segments beginning to form. Once more it arrives at a stage apparenty generically distinct from anything else, and here it was known to naturalists as *Scyphistoma*. The segments deepen, and look like a pile of saucers, each of which has serrated edges. Again it has been mistaken for another and distinct animal, and named *Strobila*. Finally, as the constriction has gone on, the segments break away, turn over, and become recognisable as true medusæ, having a diameter, however, of only the sixth of an inch, but capable of enormous growth subsequently. Their ova settle down into the small and insignificant *Hydra tuba*. Not unfrequently the phosphorescence of the sea is largely due to the immense numbers of these little medusæ.

Along the eastern and north-eastern coasts of England, there may often be met with a large jelly-fish known as *Cyanea chrysaora* (Fig. 56). This also belongs to the pulmonigrade family; and it is indeed a pretty sight to see its huge disk slowly swim by, alternately dilating and contracting as it goes. Its disk is marked with fine brown lines, which radiate from the centre, and the numerous tentacles and waving appendages suspended from the under side float gracefully to and fro. The colour of these highly attenuated organs is a faint brown, or fawn, sometimes cream-like. This species is now known to be a detached bud of a small hydrozoon. The fishermen know these jelly-fish well enough, and, for the matter of that, not a few sea-bathers also, as "Sea-nettles." This name is given them on account of the severely stinging properties which the tentacles seem to possess. Many other species of jelly-fish are endowed with this urticating property, which seems to be no mean organ of defence. Perhaps the commonest of all the naked-eyed Medusæ is the *Thaumantia*, which literally swarms in all our bays and harbours, contributing to the phosphorescence of the water. In *T. pilosella* (Fig. 57) is given the various parts of this species. Thus *a* shows the buccal arms, or oval tentacles forming the lips; and *b* the stomach. An œsophagus leads from the mouth to their gastric cavity. From its

Fig. 56.

*Cyanea chrysaora.*

upper end four gastrovascular canals (*c*) radiate towards the margin of the disk, and communicate with the circular marginal canal (*d*), which carries the nutrient fluid right round the body. On either side of the radiating canals are placed the ovaries (*e*). The action of the cilia and the motion of this nutrient fluid is beautifully shown by the microscope. The organs both of sight and hearing are believed by some naturalists to exist in these jelly-fish. *Thaumantia cymbaloidea* (Fig. 58) takes its name from its peculiar shape. In Fig. 59 we have another species of jelly-fish (*Turris digitalis*), usually brightly and even brilliantly coloured. Whilst some jelly-fish, such as the Physalia and Velella drift towards our shores from the south, the Turris visits us from the north, finding here its southern boundary. It is, however, a much smaller object

Fig. 57.

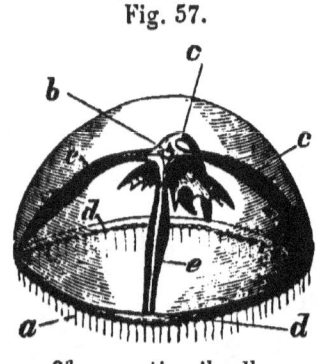

*Thaumantia pilosella.*

Fig. 58.

*Thaumantia cymbaloidea.*

than those we have been dwelling upon, and can only be obtained by a tow-net.

A pretty object, to be obtained in the same manner, is the *Sarsia*, named after the celebrated Norwegian naturalist Sars. It is exceedingly abundant in the Solent, and may be kept alive for a fortnight in a bell-glass without much trouble, thus enabling the student to become acquainted with all its habits. It is only about half an inch in height, and is deeply bell-shaped, as may be seen in Fig. 60. The upper part is thick, and the sarcode thins off along the edges. From the interior there hangs the *polypite* or stomach, like the clapper from a bell. The mouth of this organ has four lips, with which it can seize its food and take in objects, such as even the fry of fishes, much larger than its own diameter. The *Sarsia* shoots to and fro in the water by contraction, almost as rapidly as a fish swims. It has four little marginal tentacles, arising from four little tubercles, each of which bears a little

Fig. 59.

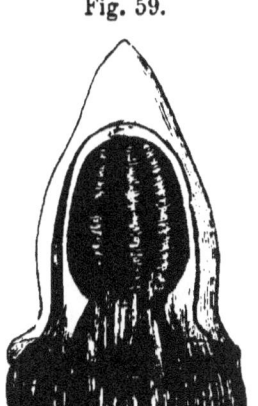

*Turris digitalis*, × 3.

Fig. 60.

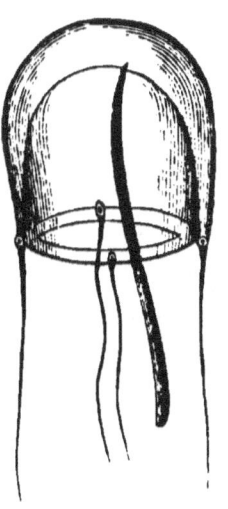

*Sarsia tubulosa*, × 2.

dark *ocellus*, or rudimentary eye-spot. The contraction is caused by four bands of fleshy tissue, some of which radiate from the centre of the bell to the margin, where they are joined by marginal bands.

Along the Devon coasts there occur other kinds of jelly-fish, seldom or never met with elsewhere in British waters. Among these is *Æquorea Forbesiana* —named after the distinguished naturalist, Professor Edward Forbes, whose work on the Medusoids is still a text-book. This species is about four inches in diameter, and an inch and a half thick, having thirty-six threadlike tentacles pendent from it. It is not so round or convex as the *Sarsia*. Like the latter, the polypite has four large lips, of a three-cornered shape, each of which is fringed along the margin. The tentacles are covered with peculiar little knobs, or swellings, capable of adhering to objects they may happen to touch. Like the tentacles of the larger jelly-fish, they possess the power of urtication, or nettling. Two species of this genus occur as far north as Ilfracombe. Their appearance is glassy above and sky-blue beneath, the radiating vessels and the lips of the polypite being of a rose-colour. Altogether it is a most beautiful object, and one not likely to be soon forgotten after it has been once identified.

Whilst speaking of these Devonshire species, we may as well mention others to be met with occasionally in the same waters, although they seem to be drifted thither by the Gulf Stream. These are the *Physalia*, or "Portuguese Man-of-war," and the *Velella*. The former is notorious for its intense stinging powers, which surpass anything yet mentioned. Its long curled tentacles whip round an object immediately, and, in the case of fishes, seem to benumb them at once. Its shape is like that of a spindle, tapering at each end, the numerous tentacles trailing behind it as it swims. Usually it makes its appearance on our coasts, not singly, but in fleets. The *Velella* is nearly allied to the above, although its shape is very different. Imagine a flat disk, thin and somewhat cartilaginous, on which another triangular disk is placed perpendicularly. Its length is about two inches, and its height one inch and a half. Its colour is fine blue, sometimes tinted with purple and green. When swimming, or rather sailing, by the aid of the vertical plate mentioned, which is acted upon by the wind, it has somewhat of a rotatory motion. The *Physalia* has no organ of locomotion whatever, but has to trust to the mercy of winds, waves, and currents; the *Velella* being little better off in this respect, as it only possesses its rudimentary sail. From the under surface of the floating disk of the latter there hangs down the polypite, and a series of marginal tentacles.

A much commoner and more thoroughly British jelly-fish is the Beröe or *Cydippe* (Fig. 61), although, singularly enough, it is structurally more nearly allied to the sea-anemones than to the medusæ. On the other hand, the *Lucernaria*, notwithstanding its sea-anemone-like appearance, is really a jelly-fish. Major Holland, speaking of the pretty Beröe, says:

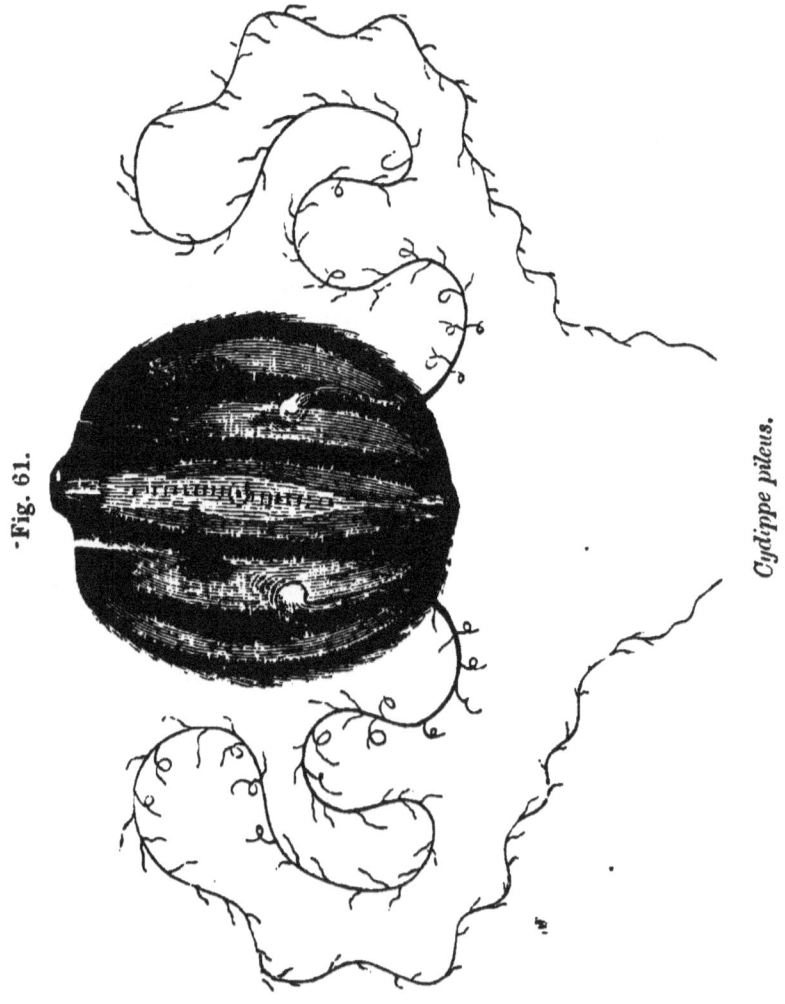

Fig. 61.

*Cydippe pileus.*

"Of all the exquisitely beautiful things that frequent our shores, none can surpass our fair *Cydippe*, one of the *ciliograde acalephæ*. If we had time we should go into raptures about the crystal globe, the eight costal bands of cilia, the long retractile tentacles, and a dozen other things! We can only remark that the learned have a grand dispute about the situation of her mouth. Reasoning from analogy, one might expect that the mouth would be situated between the tentacles at the lower pole of the globe; but Nature has thought proper to place the 'buccal' orifice at the upper, and not at the lower extremity." And yet this beautiful object is only about half an inch in diameter. Locomotion is effected by the eight ciliated bands above mentioned, each of which moves in wavy undulations, producing by the movement the most exquisite prismatic effect. The long tentacles are capable of coiling and uncoiling themselves, or can even be withdrawn into the body at pleasure. So transparent is this pretty creature, that it would sometimes not be seen in the water, except for the flashes of iridiscent light it throws off. It is in its digestive apparatus that the *Cydippe* is more nearly allied to the sea-anemones than to the true jellyfish.

The *Lucernaria* is a dark liver-coloured object, found adhering to rocks, and, in a hurry, might easily be mistaken for a peculiar sea-anemone. It is, however, nearly allied to the medusæ, and especially to that stage in their existence known as the *Hydra tuba*. It is not uncommon in our seas, and, when once pointed out, is an object not to be soon forgotten. It attaches itself to the stems of seaweeds, &c., as well as to stones; and when the former is resorted to, its appearance is not unlike the bell of the Campanula in our gardens. It can, however, detach itself at will, and even swim freely by means of the alternate contraction and expansion of its body. Round the margin of the latter are placed tufts of short tentacles, whilst in the centre is the polypite and a four-lobed mouth. When thus seen attached, it resembles in some degree an inverted medusa.

It is astonishing what a small quantity of solid matter is contained in the bodies of jelly-fishes. Wood makes the remark that they are "little else than animated sea water," and so far he is perfectly right. And yet the younger and smaller individuals contribute, in all seas, but especially in tropical, to the phenomenon known as *phosphorescence*. On some occasions they literally crowd every drop of water, and furnish inexhaustible food for myriads of other marine animals. Some species even constitute one of the staple articles of diet to the Greenland whale. As to their beauty there can only be one idea, and the disgusting grub of the painted butterfly is not more strikingly different to the parent out of whose egg it has crawled, than is the living, swimming jelly-fish to the blubber-like mass known on the beach, which has to do duty in lieu of a better acquaintance with this animal. The most learned, as well as the ignorant, stand confessed before the exquisite beauty which "animated sea water" can produce; whilst the marvellous story of alternation of generations, or metamorphoses, which we read from a careful study of this group, leads us to exclaim with Coleridge—

> "And what if all of animated Nature
> Be but organic harps, diversely framed,
> That tremble into thought, as o'er them sweeps,
> Plastic and vast, one intellectual breeze,
> At once the soul of each, and God of all!"

## VIII.

### HALF AN HOUR WITH SEA-ANEMONES.

THERE are few marine objects more deservedly popular than those to which we purpose devoting our present "half hour." Since the almost universal establishment of those charming sources of interest and amusement, marine aquaria, much greater information has been obtained as to the habits, &c., of sea-anemones. The principal writer on this subject is Mr. Gosse, whose attractive style has thrown a charm over it, and helped more than anything else to increase the number of species peculiar to Great Britain. Less than a quarter of a century ago there were only twenty-four British species known—now there are upwards of seventy. Their study in domestic aquaria has lightened many a hour of suffering and tedium, for no more beautiful creatures exist in the whole range of the animal kingdom. Well do they deserve the name which, under the Greek compounded word of *Anthozoa*, naturalists have given to them. They are, indeed, "living flowers," clad in brighter colours than the proverbial "lilies of the field," and yet exhibiting the habits, appliances, and instincts of true animals. Anemone collecting is now a recognised sea-side pursuit, and along the shores of our rockier bathing-places visitors may be seen engaged in it every day. We have already sketched forth, in our chapter on "preparations," the necessary requirements for anemone collecting, and will therefore now proceed to describe those species which the student is most likely to meet with, and whose habits are best known.

Before doing so, however, we feel sure that our readers will have their interest in anemone collecting and aquarium keeping enhanced if they know something about the zoological characters of these creatures as a class. This will be all the easier if they have read our remarks on the corallines and the jelly-fish. Sometimes the student finds the class named *Actinozoa*, or " radiated animals," from the peculiar radiating divisions of their interior. At others they may be grouped as *Zoantharia*, a word which is only the reverse of that under which we first introduced them, and signifying the same thing. Taking them altogether, we find on strict examination that the sea-anemones, or *Anthozoa*, differ from the members of the coralline and jellyfish family in having a distinct digestive sac, or stomach, situated below the body-cavity. This is separated from the outer or body wall by a space or partition, which is divided into a series of vertical compartments, like the chambers of a poppy-head. These compartments are zoologically termed " mesenteries," and their use seems to be very important in the economy of the animal. It is to their walls that the reproductive organs are attached. In the corallines these organs are always external, whilst in the anthozoa they are always internal. This is another of the marked differences separating the two classes. In the sea-anemones the reproduction is truly sexual, and appears on the chamber walls as reddish bands, filled with ova or sperm cells. Notwithstanding this sexual character, the mode of propagation seems to be *diœcious;* that is, the ova of one individual is better fertilised by the sperm of another than by its own, and *vice versâ.* The embryo, when extruded, are free-swimming, rounded bodies, furnished with the usual ciliary appendages for locomotion. Subsequently they settle down, and the tentacles develop. At first five or six only appear, but soon afterwards these numbers rapidly double themselves.

We should have stated that in the corallines, and species allied to them, the stomach, or digestive-cavity, is identical with the body-cavity. In other words, there is only one internal cavity. The animal tissues both of that group and of the sea-anemones are nearly identical; neither has any true circulatory system, or traces of nervous development. This is very remarkable, especially in the sea-anemones, whose tentacles possess a high degree of sensibility to touch, and even to light. The number of tentacles, in some species, is as great as two hundred; they generally occur in multiples of five or six, and are situated in two rows, the tentacles alternating with each other. That end of the animal on which these organs are placed is called the "disk," and that by which the entire animal attaches itself to rocks and stones, the "base." This base seems to be very sensitive to injury, although the other parts of the animal are tolerably hardy, and capable of soon recovering any damage, or even of forming two individuals out of one when torn or lacerated. The base has, in some species, the power of moving, or crawling, much like a snail, but more slowly. That part of the animal terminated at one end by the disk, and at the other by the base, is usually called the "column." This is of various lengths, in some species being very short indeed, and in others, as in the plumose anemone (*Actinoloba dianthus*, Fig. 62), very long, with a broad, flat base. The power of expansion and contraction which we noticed as peculiar to the jelly-fishes, and the means by which they progressed through the water, is possessed in a modified form by the column of the sea-anemones. Its use, as we shall see, is, however, quite different to that to which it is put in its allies. Each tentacle is hollow, and communicates with the body-cavity. By the muscular contraction of the column, the fluid in the body chambers is forced into the tentacles. The latter are thus elongated, whilst the reverse process, of course, withdraws them. Some species, as the Opelet, cannot withdraw the tentacles; but others, as the smooth anemone, do so until the creature resembles a coloured ball of jelly. Below the stomach are a series of twisted cords, called "cras-

Fig. 62.

*Actinoloba dianthus.*

peda," whose use is not clearly known, unless it be for stinging purposes. In the genus *Sagartia* the column is perforated with small holes, out of which issue stinging threads, by means of which the sea-anemones, harmless though they appear, can at once stun and paralyze their prey. Mr. Gosse describes this arrangement as follows:—" The skin of the body is pierced with minute holes, capable of being opened and closed at will, out of which can be forced curious slender threads, which lie coiled up in great profusion in the interior of the animal. These threads are almost entirely composed of those extraordinary capsules called *cnidæ*, or nettling cells, found, indeed, in most of the tissues, but nowhere in such abundance as here, which eject with amazing force a poisonous filament having the strength and elasticity of a wire, and furnished with reversed barbs, but of almost inconceivable tenuity. The filaments, projected by myriads at the pleasure of the animal, penetrate deeply into the flesh of other soft-bodied creatures, and cause immediate paralysis and sudden death." The Rev. J. G. Wood also describes these remarkable organs, which again remind us of the near relationship between the sea-anemones and the jelly-fish, the latter, it will be remembered, having this nettling power developed in the tentacles. Mr. Wood says that the capsules of the anemones are especially crowded on the tentacles, as well as scattered over various parts of the body. He tells us they " are little oval vescicles, embedded in the substance of the anemone, and containing within them a long delicate thread, closely coiled, in forms varying according to the description of capsule. The extreme tenuity of the thread may be imagined from the fact that the largest capsules are not more than the three-hundredth part of an inch in length, and that within so small a compass the thread is coiled like a watch-spring in the barrel. Indeed, the simile of a watch-spring will nearly express the object, for the thread is so strong, in spite of its tenuity, that it has been aptly compared to the main-spring of a watch. When the tentacles are irritated or compressed, myriads of these capsules start forward, become everted, and shoot forth their tiny spears. The length and shape of these wonderful filaments are very various, some being of a very great length, and so fine that a microscope of high power can hardly distinguish them; while others are only two or three times the length of the capsule that contained them, and covered with an armature of short hairs even more minute than themselves." There is, therefore, no wonder that these apparently helpless creatures should be able to feed on animals much higher in the scale than themselves, possessed, also, with powers of rapid locomotion and quickness of sight, neither of which distinguishes our sea-anemone. Strong crabs, in spite of their powerful limbs and pincers, have had to yield the ghost when they have got in the grip of these "animal flowers." Nay, it would even seem as though, in some cases, the principle of *mimicry* had had something to do with their bright colours and flower-like appearance. Thus Mr. Jonathan Couch mentions that "on one occasion, while watching a specimen that was covered merely by a film of water, a bee, wandering near, darted through the water to the mouth of the animal, evidently *mistaking* the creature for a flower; and, though it struggled a great deal to get free, was retained till it was drowned, and was then swallowed."

We now purpose dwelling briefly upon such species as the seaside visitor, under favourable circumstances, and at the proper places, may expect to find. The plumose anemone (Fig. 62, *Actinoloba dianthus*) has already been referred to. It can readily be identified from its tall column, its crown of short tentacles grouped in bunches or tufts, as well as by the thickened parapet which surrounds the column just beneath them. Its colour is very variable, sometimes being light olive, fawn-brown, orange, flesh-colour, or pure white, according to circumstances. The latter are such agencies as light and shade, and perhaps there is imported into the differences of colour an adaptation to that of the objects most numerous in the neighbourhood. This species is remarkable for its power of spontaneous division, and Mr. Gosse, speaking of this peculiarity, and alluding to the power of movement possessed by its muscular foot, says: "When a large individual has been a good while adherent to one spot, and at length chooses to change its quarters, it does so by causing its base to glide slowly along the surface on which it rests—the glass side of a tank, for instance. But it frequently happens that small, irregular fragments of the edge of the base are left behind, as if their adhesion had been so strong that the animal found it easier to tear its own tissues apart than to overcome it. The

Fig. 63.

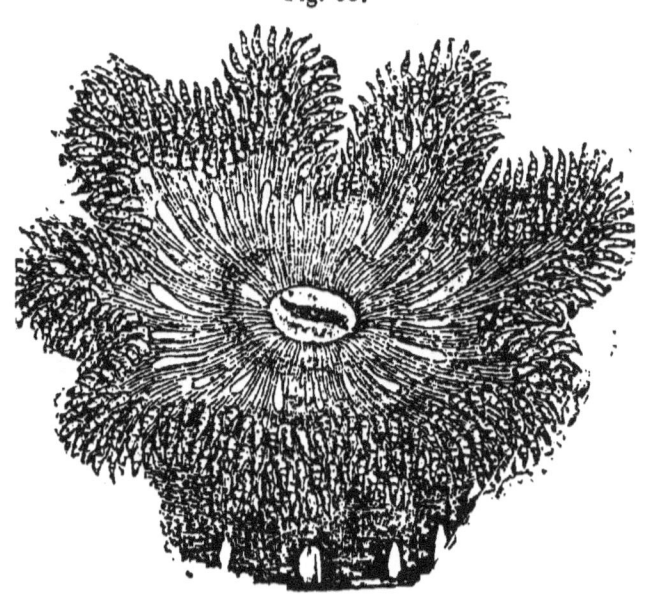

Daisy Anemone. (*Sagartia bellis*).

fragments so left soon contract, become smooth, and spherical or oval in outline, and in the course of a week or a fortnight may each be seen furnished with a margin of tentacles and a disk—transformed, in fact, into perfect though minute anemones."

The "Daisy Anemone" (Fig. 63) is a great favourite with aquarium keepers, and deservedly so.

Its generic name of *Sagartia*, given to it by Mr. Gosse, is in allusion to the method of disabling its prey, already alluded to, and is taken from the following historical fact. Herodotus informs us that in the army of Xerxes there was a certain race of warriors called "Sagartians," from their peculiar mode of fighting. When they engaged an enemy, they threw out a rope with a noose at the end. Anything a Sagartian caught, whether horse or man, was dragged towards himself, and those entangled in the coils were speedily put to death. From what has been said, it will be seen that there is something more than mere poetical figure in thus giving to the "Daisy" its generic name. Along the coasts of Devon and Cornwall, the "Daisy Anemone" is very abundant, the rock-pools being literally lined with it, as its terrestrial namesake carpets the fields in May. A curious habit possessed by it is that of being able to elongate one of its tentacles to a great length, whilst the others remain of the ordinary dimensions. Nearly allied to the "Daisy" is the "Cave Anemone" (Fig. 64), a name it well deserves from its hermit-like habits. It is one of the most variable of all our British sea-anemones, more than twenty varieties of colours having been published. It is also one of the most abundant and widely distributed of all the species. And yet, in spite of its great variability, there is very little difficulty in determining and recognising it. A characteristic mark is usually present on the tentacles, greatly resembling the letter B, as may be seen in Fig. 65. The tentacles of the "Cave Anemone" are numerous, often more than two hundred being present on a single specimen. Its Greek name of *Troglodytes* is in allusion to the same habit as is expressed in its common English one.

Fig. 64.

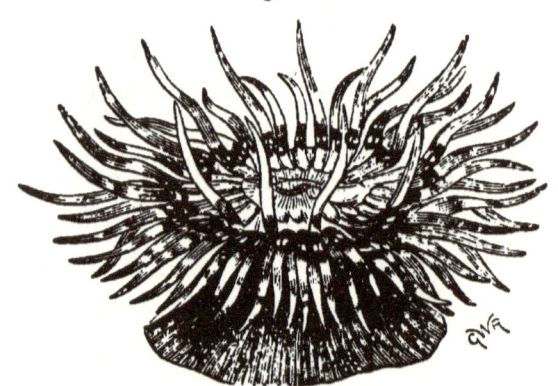

"Cave Anemone." (*Sagartia troglodytes*).

Fig. 65.

When placed in an aquarium, however, it loses a great deal of the apparent moroseness which has caused it to be thus designated, and behaves pretty much as its brother anemones do.

Two rarer species, the "Rosy Anemone" (*Sagartia rosea*) and the "Orange-Disked Anemone" (*Sagartia venusta*) are usually great favourites with aquarium keepers. Speaking of the former,

Mr. Gosse, in his enthusiastic style, exclaims: "When left by the receding tide, it protrudes from its tiny cavity in the overhanging rock, and droops a pear-shaped button of orange brown, with a cluster of brilliant purple tentacles just showing their tips from the half-opened centre, and a drop of water sparkling like a dewdrop hanging from them." The "Rosy Anemone" usually frequents holes in the rock, so that its capture is attended with no little difficulty. When describing its appearance and colour more in detail, Mr. Gosse says: "It has a firm fleshy column of Sienna brown, paler towards the base, and with the upper part studded with indistinct spots, marking the situation of certain organs which have an adhesive power. The disk is of a pale neutral tint, with a crimson mouth in the centre, and a circumference of crowded tentacle, of the most lovely rose-purple, the rich hue of that lovely flower that bears the name of General Jacqueminot. In those specimens that are most widely opened this tentacular fringe forms a blossom whose petals overhang the concealed column, expanding to the width of an inch or more; but there are others in which the expansion is less complete in different degrees, and these all give distinct phases of loveliness. We find a few among the rest which, with the characteristically coloured tentacles, have the column and disk of a creamy white, and one in which the disk is of a brilliant orange, inclining to scarlet. Most lovely little creatures

K

are they all!" The "Orange-Disked Anemone" (*Sagartia venusta*) is found in various places along the south and west coasts of Great Britain and Ireland, and is remarkable for its bright orange disk and snow-white tentacles. It is usually found in colonies, thus differing from the "Cave Anemone." Specimens may sometimes be obtained an inch and a half in diameter when the tentacles are expanded. This species is perhaps the most lovely of all our native sea-anemones, and when seen in its healthy condition, the most matter-of-fact philosopher might be tempted to pardon the enthusiastic admiration of anemone collectors for it. The "Parasitic Anemone" (*Sagartia parasitica*, Fig. 66) is often found in large numbers where it does occur. It takes its name from its habit of attaching itself to some shell, generally to that of the common cockle, as shown in Fig. 66. It is also found on dead shells, especially on those inhabited by the Hermit-crab, and in this respect much resembles the *Adamsia*. It is a species which thrives very well in the aquarium, where it will leave the shell, and attach itself to the glass. One good distinguishing mark of this species, besides its parasitic habit and striped

Fig. 66.

Parasitic Anemone
(*Sagartia parasitica*).

body, is a dark line which runs down each side of every tentacle.

The anemone just referred to, the *Adamsia*, is very remarkable on account of its always being found in company with a species of Hermit-crab. It lives in deep water, and Mr. Gosse remarks that he believed there was no instance on record of its living without the crab, or the crab without it. One which he had in his aquarium thus in partnership, was taken off the shell in which the Hermit crab lived, but before long they were found together again. At length he observed the crab (after another divorce) take the anemone up with its claws, and gently apply it to the mouth of the shell in which it lived, the anemone being evidently favourable to the operation, for there it afterwards remained. We have heard of strange attachments between horses and dogs, but it is indeed singular to find such a union between a soft-bodied crab and a sea-anemone! The reason for this strange union is quite a puzzle to naturalists, but there can be little doubt it is mutually advantageous in some way or another.

The "Opelet" (*Anthea cereus*, Fig. 67) is so called on account of its inability to withdraw its snake-like tentacles. It is not an uncommon species on rockbound coasts, and may be found in many rock-pools between tides. It adheres by a broad base to the rocks, or to the larger tangles. The poisoning powers are very highly developed in this species, so that it is very fatal to small fishes, &c., in the aquarium. Another remarkable feature about it is that it occasionally splits itself into two individuals. The reader cannot fail to identify it by its dark olive-green tentacles, and their incapability of retraction; so that it would seem as if their colour atoned for this defect, and assimilated it to the surrounding seaweeds.

Fig. 67.

"Opelet" anemone (*Anthea cereus*).

The "Beadlet Anemone" (*Actinia mesembryanthemum*, Fig. 68) is just the reverse of the Opelet, for no other anemone has such thoroughly retractile tentacles. When they are withdrawn, the creature looks to all the world like a globular mass of jelly, or, as Mr. Gosse describes it, "like ripe fruits, so plump, and succulent, and glossy, and high-coloured, that we are tempted to stretch forth the willing hand, to pluck and eat." This species is without doubt the most abundant in our British seas, and

Fig. 68.

Beadlet (*Actinia mesembryanthemum*).

the seaside visitor, who looks well into the rockpools at low water, is sure to capture as many specimens as he will care to carry away. It is a species, also, which multiplies rapidly in the aquarium; whilst it is certainly the oldest liver, and the most *hardy*. The Rev. J. G. Wood relates an instance of the latter quality worth repeating. He says: "A gentleman had brought some of them to town with him, and had been examining them in company with a friend. After the examination, supper was brought in by an unsophisticated servant, and removed by the same individual. While the table was being cleared, the servant asked what was to be done with the anemones, and was told to put them carefully away in a jug. Now the only jug at that time on the table was a jug containing porter, and into that jug the anemones were severally dropped. About a fortnight afterwards the anemones were again called into requisition, and the jug demanded. Great was the astonishment of their owner to see the porter jug produced, and still greater when he found the creatures were still living!" As illustrative of the longevity of the "Beadlet," Mr. Lloyd mentions one individual in an aquarium in Edinburgh, which has lived there more than forty-four years, and during that period produced more than a thousand young. It is still healthy, and seems as likely to live another forty years. Its name of "Beadlet" is given to it on account of the rows of bright blue beads at the base of the tentacles. They are most striking and beautiful ornaments, and the student cannot fail to recognise this species by them alone. The following is Mr. Gosse's glowing description of this "common object of the seashore." "Some are greengages, some Orleans plums, some magnumbonums, so various are their rich hues; but look beneath the water, and you see them not less numerous, but of quite another guise. These are all widely expanded, the tentacles are thrown out in an arch over the circumference, leaving a broad flat disk, just like a many-petalled flower of gorgeous hues; indeed we may fancy that here we see the blossoms, and there a ripened fruit. Do not omit, however, to notice the beads of pearly blue that stud the margin all around, at the base of the overarching tentacles."

The "Dahlia Wartlet Anemone" (*Tealia crassicornis*, Fig. 69) is another very abundant British species, and without doubt the largest and finest of the group, some being found of the size of an ordinary cheese-plate. Its name is well deserved, for none of the anemones look more like a flower than does this species when its tentacles are fully expanded; and of all flowers, it seems to resemble that which has given to it its name the most. It is abundant on every rocky coast, at or near the verge of low water, and may be seen left dry, when numbers of them huddle together, their stomachs extended, forming most unsightly objects, which contrast strongly with their lovely, flower-like appearance when covered by water. The "Dahlia Anemone" has a habit of covering its body with large grains of sand, pebbles, or fragments of shells, so that, apart from its great size, this is a good means of recognising it. It is extremely sensitive on its basal portion, the slightest injury frequently causing

Fig. 69.

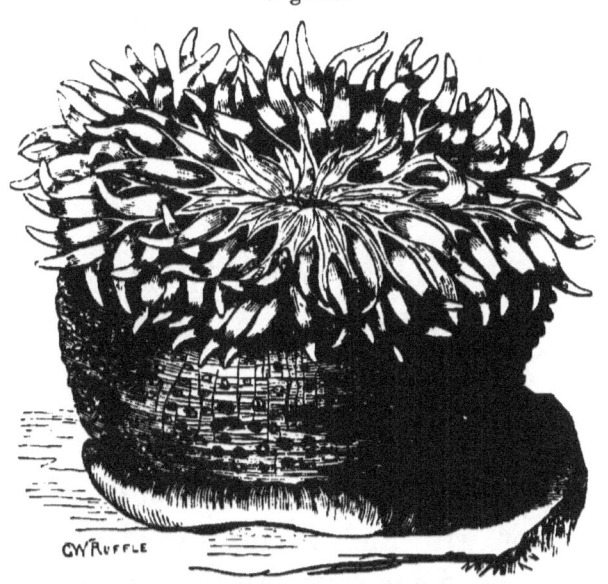

Dahlia Wartlet (*Tealia crassicornis*).

death. Its great voracity—illustrated by Mr. Wood, who watched one individual catch and swallow two small crabs in a very short time—renders it unfit for a general aquarium, an objection which its great size further bears out. But it may be kept in separate glass tanks, and fed with pieces of meat, &c., when it seems to take to its new home very

# 136 HALF AN HOUR WITH SEA-ANEMONES.

readily. It was this species to which Mr. Couch referred, when he related the anecdote of a bee mistaking it for a flower.

The limits of inexorable space oblige us to conclude our introduction to the sea-anemones with a reference to a peculiar and distinct variety of the "Opelet," commonly known as the "Strawberry Anemone." For size, it may sometimes compete with the "Dahlia." It is not so common, however, as the latter, although when it is met with it is generally in abundance.' It occurs nearer to low

Fig. 70.

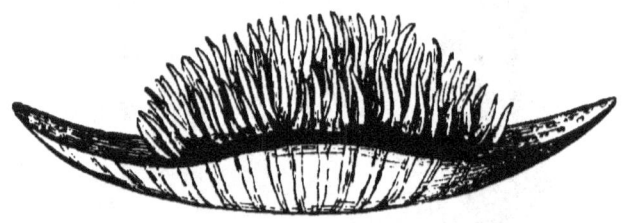

"Strawberry" anemone.

water mark than the normal form of "Opelet," and the collector will find it readily yield when he endeavours to detach its base from the rocks or stones. The "Strawberry Anemone" is the most easily kept of all, and is a great ornament to the aquarium, creeping about the side of the tank, and expanding its base into an irregularly elliptical form, as seen in Fig. 70. When thus expanded, it has been seen to attain a length of five inches. Many others of our native species we are obliged to pass over, but those who feel disposed to enter more fully upon the study of these pretty and pleasing objects, cannot do better than get Mr. Gosse's "Sea-anemones," a book that will be sure to please them, as much for the charming style in which it is written, as for its intimate acquaintance with the objects on which it treats. Sea-anemone collecting has this advantage over many others—its objects cannot fail to elicit general admiration when transferred to the bell-glass or aquarium, and hence one more readily gets the sympathies of one's friends.

## IX.

### HALF AN HOUR WITH SEA-MATS AND SQUIRTS.

A TRUE naturalist can sympathise with the theories of the early Greek philosophers, who taught that the sea was the great menstruum of life, and its slime the ultimate and original basis of life. Indeed, we do not seem to have got far from this early theory, for the modern doctrine of protoplasm carries it out theoretically, and its application to the sarcodous masses called *Bathybius*, lying along the deeper parts of the sea bottom, makes us admire all the more the keen intellect of those old Greek guessers of natural phenomena. But even if we were without such evidence of the shrewdness of the hypothesis, the abundance of life which peoples every drop of sea-water would cause us to regard it as poetically true. Life on the dry land is marvellously developed, especially plant life, in its many phases, from the lichen to the oak. But we find in the sea that a corresponding series of changes are rung in the animal world. From the scarcely animated jelly of the *Bathybius*, to the whale, there is a wonderful series of organic forms, living not only now, but in the past ages of the earth's history, which graduate into each other in the most marvellous fashion. There is a scientific truth underlying

Pope's well-known lines, such as the poet then little dreamt of.

"All are but parts of one harmonious whole,
Whose body Nature is, and God the soul."

The study of natural history is in the direction of filling up the supposed "gaps" in this "harmonious whole," and every discovery is decidedly in favour of this idea, in spite of the ignorant cry about "missing links." If we knew all that could be known about the animals and plants that have lived, as well as those which still live, such a cry might be respected as having something in it. But science has not yet got to the end of its tether, nor is it likely it soon will be. Until then, therefore, we should advise such alarmists to adopt a prudent silence, more especially as the progress of scientific discovery is so decidedly against them.

That excessive abundance of life which caused the ancient philosophers to regard the sea with such reverence, can be authenticated by the seaside visitor at almost every step he takes along the shore. There is not a seaweed thrown up after a night's storm that is not a *microcosm*, a "little world" of its own, crowded with life forms. The rock-pools are miniature universes, in which the balance of the animal and vegetable kingdoms is kept up, as if there were not another square yard on the surface of the earth that was inhabited. Hence there need be no dearth in objects of interest to the student of marine zoology or botany. We have endeavoured to describe some of the commonest objects of the seashore, and now proceed to notice others about which there prevails a universal mistake. The seaside visitor will have observed that the long fronds of many of the larger seaweeds are frequently coated over with beautiful and delicate lace-like objects, which sometimes cover the entire surface. No one who has seen these elegant objects can help wondering what they are. Again, there may be picked up, along the margin of high-water, bunches of seaweed-like objects, which, however, seem drier, and rustle more stiffly than seaweeds are wont to do. Still, their leaf, or frond-like appearance, would lead even intelligent people to conclude they were some kind of seaweeds. At other times the stems and branches of real seaweeds seem to be parasitically overburdened with similar objects adhering to them. It is with these peculiar forms that we have now to do, and with others, shortly to be described, that are zoologically related to them. Their popular name is "sea-mosses," or "sea-mats," the latter in allusion to the way in which they cover or mat the surfaces of the large fronds of seaweeds. Instead of being vegetables, however, or at all related to them, these "sea-mats" are *animals*, or, rather, colonies of animals, and that of a highly endowed and specialised kind. Fig. 71 will furnish the reader with a good idea of the general appearance of these "sea-mats," whilst Fig. 72 gives a magnified illustration of the reticulated appearance of the fronds when seen

HALF AN HOUR WITH SEA-MATS AND SQUIRTS. 141

with a strong lens. Before describing them in detail, however, it will be as well to keep to our plan of explaining, as briefly as possible, the position of the group in the animal kingdom, and the characters which distinguish it.

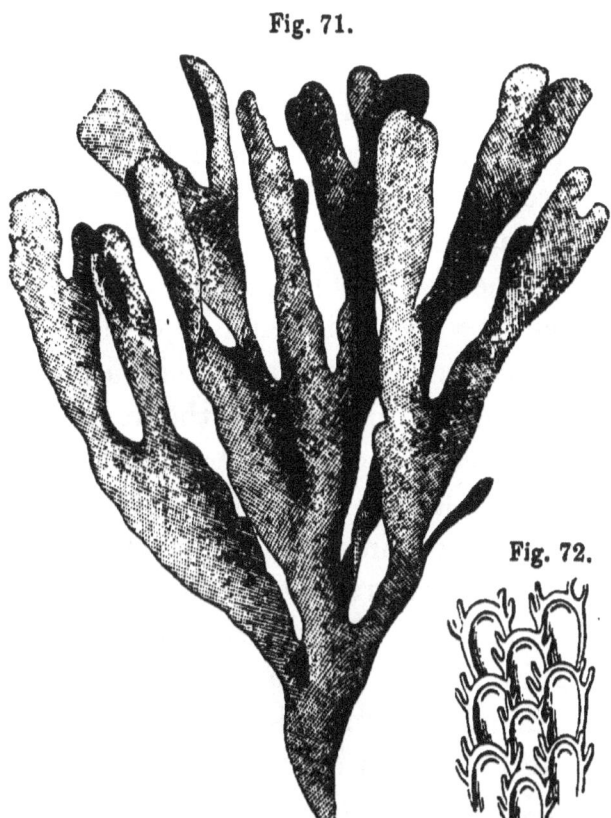

Fig. 71.

Fig. 72.

Sea-Mat (*Flustra hispida*).    Ditto, magnified.

The magnified representation already given shows the surfaces of the fronds to be covered with a network of chambers. These chambers have walls of a horny substance, in which there is often diffused carbonate of lime to strengthen them. The chambers have each a small semicircular aperture, in which the animal formerly lived, and out of which it could thrust its tentacles or cilia. The scientific name given to this group is *Polyzoa*, or "many creatures;" sometimes we find them called *Bryozoa*, or "moss-like animals." Singularly enough, these apparently insignificant creatures are nearly allied to shell-fish, and are much more highly organized than the corallines, with which they were formerly classed on account of both having a horny or *chitinous* framework. The distinction between the two classes is very great, and especially in their internal structure. In the corallines, already dwelt upon, we have shown that all the individuals are united by a common flesh, scientifically termed *cœnosarc*. The latter, however, is only a technical Greek word signifying the same thing. In the sea-mats, on the contrary, the connection is merely an *external* one, and the various species rarely are connected in any other manner. A distinct and separate animal lives in each net-like chamber, and has no connection with its neighbour except that of simple contact. In spite of this distinctive fact, the entire colony has in every case been developed from a single individual. To distinguish the individuals of a colony, like those of the sea-mat in Fig. 71, the name of *Polypide* has been given them, *Polypite* being the technical name of each member of the colony in the sea-firs, or corallines.

We have already referred to the comparatively highly endowed character of these minute creatures. When microscopically examined, each individual is seen to be enclosed in a double walled bag or sac, of which the outer one is the horny case to be seen in dried specimens. The inner wall is membranaceous, and has two openings, one of which is the mouth and the other the anus. The former is surrounded by cilia or tentacles, by means of which the animal not only breathes, as with gills, but also produces currents in the sea-water, which bring to it its food. Both the mouth and tentacles can be wholly or partially withdrawn into the aperture, by means of a muscle provided for the purpose. When obtained alive, a colony like that of the *Flustra hispida* (Fig. 71), after it has been plunged into fresh sea-water, seems to interpose a pale, thin cloud betwixt its irregular surface and the spectator's eye. Let the vessel in which it has been placed, however, receive a shock, and this cloud is instantaneously dispelled. The cloudy appearance has been produced by the ciliated animals, which had been drawn out of their cells to revel in the fresh sea-water, and the misty shade by the movement of their ciliæ. So timid and highly endowed with caution are these minute animals, that they sink into concealment on the apprehension of danger, and show by their reappearance their relief from alarm. Some naturalists are of opinion that this extreme sensitiveness partakes much of the character of that which gives to the *mimosa* leaves the popular name of "sensitive plant." So beautifully constructed is their outer coat, that even long after the animals have died, and the cells are empty, they form most attractive objects for the microscope.

Examined minutely, the mouth of each polypide is found to pass into a gullet, and thence into a stomach, through the intestines, and out at the anus. The reproductive organs are distinct, male and female, in each individual. In them, also, we get the first trace of a nervous system, which is generally absent in the corallines and jelly-fish. New individuals are produced by "budding," as well as by sexual reproduction, the latter remaining attached to its parent, and thus forming a colony; whilst the ova settle down individually, and so lay the foundations of another settlement. We should add that, on account of the general structural resemblance of these creatures to the bivalve shellfish, and especially to that order of the latter known as the *Brachiopoda*, they are grouped under the name of *Molluscoid*, or "mollusc-like" animals. They have been in existence for a long period of time, as we find the remains of their empty cells in the rocks of nearly every geological formation.

One species we have already drawn attention to, and in Fig. 73 is another and nearly allied one. This and *Flustra foliacea* are perhaps the commonest in our native seas, and may be found thrown up

HALF AN HOUR WITH SEA-MATS AND SQUIRTS. 145

after every storm. In the winter they are especially abundant, and on some parts of our coasts they

Fig. 73.

*Flustra truncata*, nat. size.

Fig. 74.

Portion of same, × 60.

might then be gathered by the cart-load. Fig. 74 is a magnified representation of the last-named species, showing that even when dead and dried up it forms

L

an object of no mean beauty. Fig. 75 introduces us to yet another species of this common

Fig. 75.

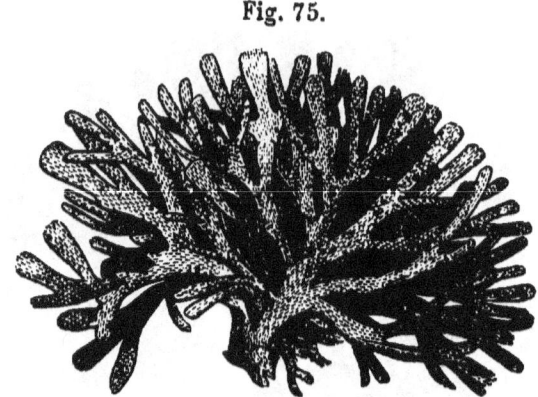

*Flustra chartacea.*

genus, which, however, has not quite so wide-spread a geographical distribution, being more abundant on our southern and south-eastern coasts than elsewhere. It is a more delicate and fragile specimen, its fronds also being smaller and more tufted. A portion of the same, magnified sixty diameters, is given in Fig. 76.

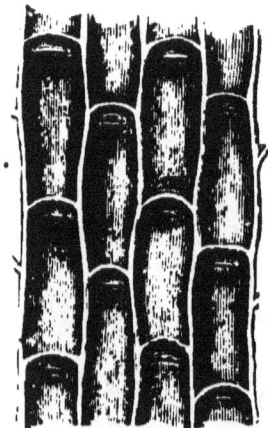

Fig. 76.

Portion of same, × 60.

We now turn to another genus, nearly allied to the above, whose chief feature is the necessity it seems under of attaching itself to some other body, as the fronds and stems of seaweeds, or even the surfaces of shells, &c. The apertures are

HALF AN HOUR WITH SEA-MATS AND SQUIRTS. 147

defended by long, bristle-like hairs, which remain some time after the colony is dead. Fig. 77 will easily introduce a specimen to the eye of the reader. Another species of the same genus is also to be found

Fig. 77.

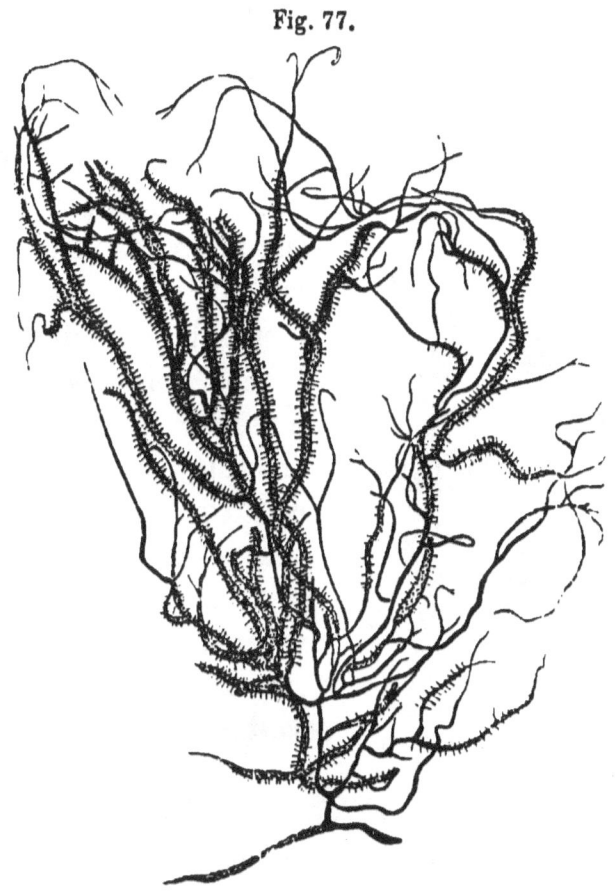

*Membranipora pilosa* encrusting sea-weed, nat. size.

matting the surfaces of the larger fronds of seaweeds, often their whole length. The cell-cases in this genus are comparatively larger than those of the last, as is shown in Fig. 78, where the position of the spines or bristly hairs is also given.

We now come to another division of the Molluscoidea, common in British seas, and some of the members of which our readers cannot fail to be introduced to in the course of their seaside rambles. This division is called *Tunicata*, on account of the bodies of some of the animals being enveloped in a leathery integument, which is called a "test," and takes the place of the ordinary shells of a bivalve. Inside this is another membrane, which possesses a muscular power of contracting, and, in doing so, can squirt or force out the sea-water. Hence the popular name of "sea-squirts" is given to these animals. They are found solitarily inhabiting a stone or a rock, in twos and threes, and also in colonies. Many of them are so like the sewn wine-skins still in use in eastern countries for bottles, that they go by the term *Ascidians* (from "askos," a wine-skin). The two openings stick out, and cause the resemblance to be very striking. Like the Polyzoan animals just mentioned, the Ascidians have the mouth opening into a respiratory cham-

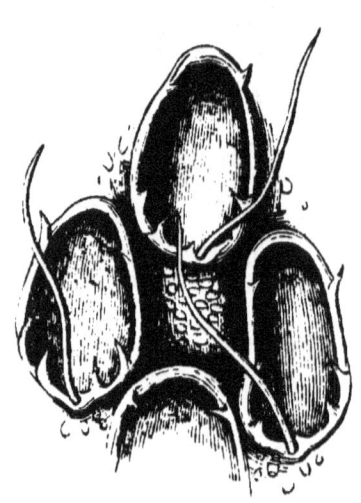

Fig. 78.

*Membranipora pilosa*, × 60.

ber, have a gullet, stomach, and intestines communicating with the anal aperture. In them, also, we get a simple, rudimentary heart; and although there is no real blood, as in the higher animals, this heart causes the circulating fluid "to ebb and flow like the tide," as Dr. S. P. Woodward describes it. In this way the two ends of the heart are alternately arterial and venous. The nervous system is represented by a ganglion, or nerve-centre. The reproductive organs, situated in a fold of the intestines, are male and female, combined in the same individual. The embryos, or young, are free-swimming animals, with a long tail like a tadpole. To the celebrated John Hunter is due the discovery that these creatures were nearly allied to the mollusca, and old Aristotle — whose zoological researches modern science has proved to be so far ahead of his time, remarks of them: "They are the only kind of mollusca whose whole body is enclosed in the shell, and that shell of a substance between true shell and leather; it may be cut like dry leather.

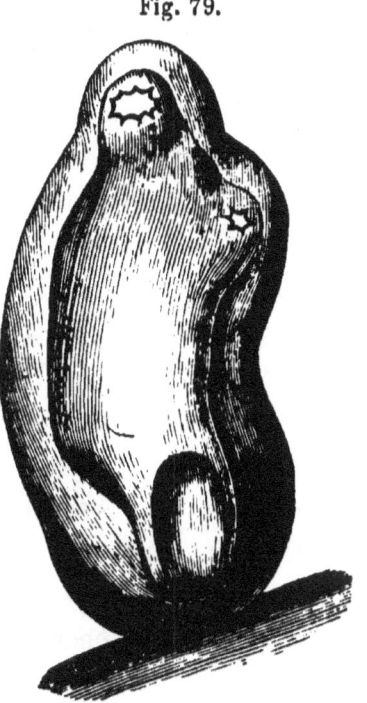

Fig. 79.

*Ascidia mentula.*

If we open them, we find a nervous membrane lining this leathery case, and fixed to it at two points, corresponding to the two separate openings, the one to take in, the other to eject the water." In this respect, the anal and mouth tubes correspond to the siphons we see in such bivalve shells as Venus. In Fig. 79 we have an illustration of the commonest and most abundant of our British species, which, however, can only be met with in tolerably deep water, and therefore must be looked for in the rubbish brought in by the trawling-boats. It ranges in depth from low water to about twenty fathoms, being most abundant off the mouths of large rivers, where it is so common as to fill the nets of the fishermen, and cause them no small annoyance. Although attached by its base to some object along the sea-bottom, it is easily loosened, especially by such a powerful implement as the trawl. Mr. Wood describes them as "looking to all the world like white hot-house grapes," when first brought up. With many of the fishermen the belief is strong that they are nothing more or less than congealed water! One very striking peculiarity belongs to the Ascidians—the outer tunic or coat contains a substance called *cellulose*, which was before deemed peculiar to the vegetable kingdom, and indeed has only been found out of it in this animal. Dr. Woodward thinks it may be due to the fact the Ascidians feed on diatoms and minute vegetation. The same coat also contains rude spicules or concretions, like those found in Gorgonias and "dead men's fingers" (*Alcyonium*). Within the last few months an additional interest has been given to these creatures through Darwin, in his " Descent of Man," speculating that evolution, or development, has proceeded direct from them up to man. It is in allusion to this hypothesis that Major Holland humorously remarks : " Now take off your hats, and behold in reverent silence the unchanged descendants of the first vertebrate progenitors of the human race. These are old-fashioned fellows, who have not departed from the customs of their forefathers. Ages ago, some adventurous speculators developed themselves desperately, and their progeny are now kings, and bishops, and judges, and no one knows what; but these are the offspring of steady-going old ' square-toes,' who clung to the good old ways of the good old times ! They hated 'selection,' and eschewed development; this is the reason why they are still *Ascidians*, and instead of 'saving' France or 'unificating' Germany, they are being dragged up by the trawl, and put into a pickle-bottle !" There are no fewer than nineteen species of Ascidia found in British seas. One (*Ascidium echinatum*) may be readily identified by the numerous conical projections on the surface, each of which has a bunch of radiating bristles.

In many respects the next genus, *Cynthia*, is nearly allied to the foregoing. The illustration in Fig. 80, of *Cynthia rustica*, will show the same arrangement of mouth and arms. It may easily be recognised by the syphon being four-cornered, instead of folded. The same Fig. shows the tadpole-like young of this creature. By-and-by the tail becomes absorbed, and the young animal, which had previously swum by a series of jerks of the tail, is obliged to settle down to the staid and steady habits of its parents. The "Currant-squirter," as Mr. Gosse calls another species (*C. grossularia*), may be found in deepish water, adhering to pebbles, shells, &c. It greatly resembles, when its tubes are withdrawn, the red, pellucid fruit which has given to it its name; and this comparison is further assisted by its size, which is about that of a red currant. Another species (*Cynthia quadrangularis*) is much larger, being frequently found two inches high. It looks much like soft leather, and in its shape is nearly square. The external is often covered with extraneous objects, and is furrowed and roughened so as to resemble kangaroo leather. Cynthia is thus found solitary, and in small numbers.

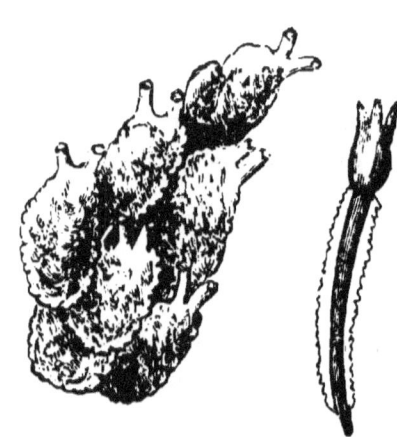

Fig. 80.

*Cynthia*, and its Tadpole.

The next group of Ascidians is extremely common, and the student will find it on the fronds of almost every specimen of the larger seaweeds. It is called *Botryllus*—a Greek word signifying a bunch of grapes—on account of the animals being connected with each other, much like a bunch of grapes, on a stem. Take a piece of rock or weed thus encrusted with what seem *stars* set in jelly, and place it in your bell-glass. Immediately you see the beautiful little stars, five to nine-rayed, but whose prevailing number is seven. These are partially imbedded in and held together by the dull slimy skin. Each star is a family, each group of stars a community, and each ray of every star a distinct individual, containing in its innermost recesses all the machinery of life, the respiratory gill-plates and circulatory pumps, which a microscopic investigation can discern to be producing minute whirlpools, taking in and throwing out the currents of water needful to the animal's existence. Round each star, as if marking out the rays more distinctly, is a band of deep purple colour, which gives the stars the appearance of being raised in relief. Six species of this beautiful genus are described as occurring in British seas. Fig. 81 will give the reader a good idea of the general appearance of these interesting objects. Perhaps the most beautiful of all the species is *Botryllus violaceus*, which has six- and seven-rayed stars of a dark blue colour.

Allied to the above are several other genera, such as *Clavelina, Lepralia*, and *Perophora*, some of which may be seen like little gelatinous threads extending over stones, &c. Every now and then the zigzag thread expands into a little cup, variously coloured, which is the true ascidian. In many respects Lepralia seems allied to the sea-mats, and its stony scurf may be seen covering seaweeds. When examined with magnifying glass, it is a very beautiful object. But, perhaps the most curious of all, is that

Fig. 81.

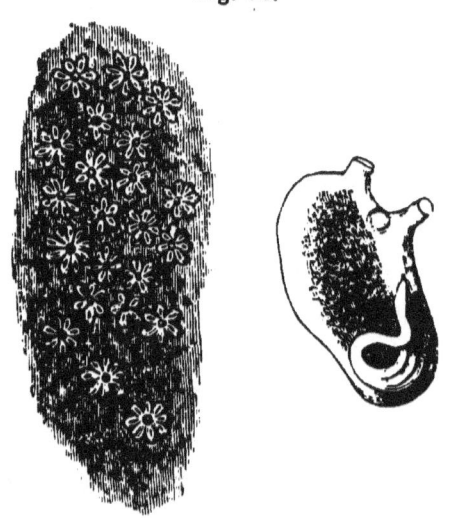

*Botryllus polycyclus.*

known as the *Salpa*, in which we have the principal of alternation of generation carried out very fully. The first discoverer of this peculiarity, Chamisso, was ridiculed and laughed at when he made it known to the world. But "they laugh most who win," and Chamisso's discovery has since been abundantly verified. In the words of that naturalist, "a *salpa* mother does not resemble her own daughter or mother, but her sister, her granddaughter, and her grandmother!" The young of these animals form long chains, many feet in length, which swim with a rhythmical serpentine motion, and at night may be traced by the phosphorescent light they give out. The adult individuals seem to prefer a separate and more or less solitary existence. Formerly, one stage in the life-history of the *salpa* was believed to be a distinct animal, just such a mistake as we have seen to be caused by a similar alternation in the corallines. Truly, the more we investigate the natural history economy of the animal world, the more profoundly ignorant do we feel; and his must be a strangely constituted mind that, in the presence of such numerous and wondrous facts, does not feel awe-inspired, as if in the very presence-chamber of the Deity.

## X.

### HALF AN HOUR WITH SEA-URCHINS AND STAR-FISH.

ALTHOUGH the animals on which we propose to treat in the present chapter are more of a deep sea character than the rest, the seaside visitor cannot fail to come across specimens. The well-known star-fishes are indeed commonly thrown ashore, and, to all appearance, dead. Should the visitor, as we have repeatedly advised him, look out for the trawl-boats as they come in, or bribe the fishermen to put aside their "rubbish" for him, he will soon be in no want of objects to illustrate our remarks. At low water, also, under the stones, he may find, when he has turned them over, the sea-urchins and star-fish of certain species lurking there, and quietly waiting the tide to flow over and give them a chance of extending their knowledge of the world, and getting another meal!

The structure both of star-fishes and sea-urchins is very remarkable, and cannot fail to elicit expressions of admiration. Notwithstanding the apparent unlikeness of these two groups of marine animals, there is actually little difference. Both are constructed pretty much on the same plan, whilst the internal arrangement is still more striking. These animals, along with others, were formerly grouped by Cuvier under the sub-kingdom of "Radiata;" and we still hear these spoken of as "radiate" animals, a term we can readily understand if we take the common star-fish as a type. But modern science has rearranged the animal kingdom, and learned to look more deeply than at superficial resemblances for their true relationships. Hence the name of "Annuloida" is now given to the star-fishes, sea-urchins, and sea-cucumbers (*Holothuria*).

To look at the seemingly inert star-fish, or the bristly sea-urchin, whose appearance has evidently given to it its common name, on account of its resemblance to the Hedgehog, one would never dream of the marvellous hydraulic machinery by means of which they are enabled to move about, any more than we should imagine them to be the terribly carnivorous creatures they are. We will take one of the spiny sea-urchins first—such an one as you may obtain from the trawl-boat, or as you may chance to find yourself underneath the stones, as *Echinus miliaris*. The spines render them as difficult to handle as their terrestrial namesakes are for dogs to worry. But if you drop it in fresh-water, the creature soon dies, and you then find that the spines, and the membranaceous skin at their bases, will peel off, leaving a tubercled shell beneath, which is very pretty to look at. Each one of these rounded tubercles acted as a joint, to which the cup-shaped hollow of each spine was attached, thus giving each spine the utmost freedom of motion. The shell, or "test" as it is usually called, is composed of pieces of carbonate of lime, of which there are no fewer than six hundred that go to make up the whole, like a piece of beautiful mosaic-work. And yet this same shell, which may be two or three inches in diameter, is fundamentally the same as that possessed by it when it was not so large as a pea! How, then, has it grown to its present size? When the process is explained, our readers cannot refrain from an expression of wonder at this additional instance of the Creator's wisdom. We mentioned the membrane that lines the outside of the shell—this has the power of secreting carbonate of lime from the sea-water, and it is somehow inserted between and around every one of the six hundred pieces that make up the whole structure. Hence each of these can only grow along *its edges*, by the addition of lime, and, as all grow slowly alike, the shell thus gradually enlarges itself to suit the requirements of the soft-bodied parts within, and which it is called upon to protect.

The physiological organization of the *Echinoderms*, as these creatures are also called, in allusion to their "spiny skins," is much higher than might at first be supposed. The sea-urchin, for instance, has a mouth and anus, an alimentary canal, and a distinct nervous system. But by far the most singular part of its organization is that termed the "water vascular" system, by means of which all the Echinodermata are enabled to move about. Among the rest of the plates which build up the solid shell, are some called the "genital-plates." On one of these is placed the "madreporiform tubercle," which is perforated, and seems to act as a filter to allow the water to pass through, but to prevent any solid bodies entering with it. A canal proceeds, internally, from this tubercle to a central tube which forms a ring round the gullet: thence proceed five canals, radiating like the arms of a star-fish, and passing along the interior until they meet at the top of the shell. Each canal gives off a series of short tubes in its course. Supposing the student had emptied the sea-urchin of its internal soft parts, as well as deprived it of its outer skin and spines, he would then have seen, by holding the hollow and empty shell up to the light, that it was constructed of ten zones of plates, five of which were perforated all the way up by rows of minute holes. Well, the tubes given off by the internal canals which we just mentioned pass through these holes, minute though they be; so minute, indeed, that the point of the finest needle would more than fill one. In this way, the tubes gain access to the outer world. At their bases, on the other side the canal, is a little water-bag connected with them. This has a muscular power, and when it contracts the result is to elongate the tube very much, and thus force it outside the shell. These tubes are called "ambulacral" feet, and each one is provided with a sucker at its end, so that it can attach itself to a surface. A few scores thus attached will warp or pull the body of the sea-urchin along. Long though the spines are, the sucking feet can be thrust forth further still, and, as the animal can put them forth at will in any direction, and retract them in the same easy way, it follows that it can crawl or warp itself along over the sea-bottom wherever it chooses! Even

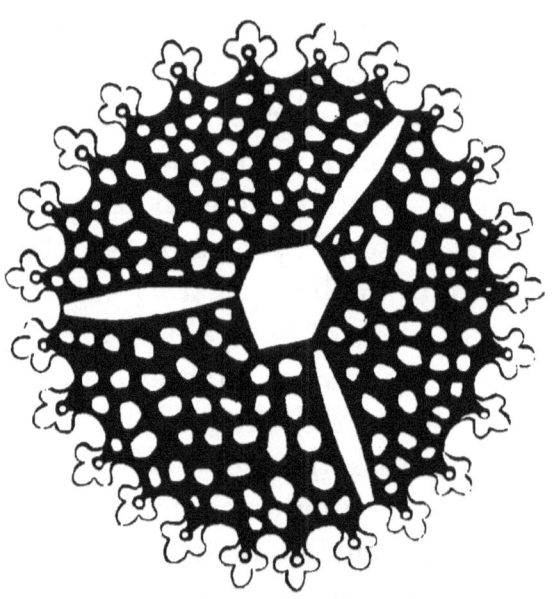

Ambulacral Disc, × 180.

these suckers have a calcareous skeleton, which forms a beautiful microscopical object, as may be seen in Fig. 82.

The mouth of the sea-urchin is very peculiar, and well adapted for trituration. Just within it may be seen five conical teeth, which are formed of lime, and all come to a point so as to form a cone. Their bases are inside the shell, and each tooth has a peculiar loop and plates, by which the muscles are able to work it. These teeth can be taken out altogether after the animal is dead, when they present a very peculiar appearance, all of them adhering together. From their curious form, their combined skeleton was compared by Aristotle to a lantern, and hence naturalists have christened it the "Lantern of Aristotle." Most probably, the visitor will pick up this skeleton separately, in his walks along the shore, as it is by no means an uncommon object, and soon gets loose from the interior of the echinus shell after the animal is dead. The teeth somewhat resemble the front teeth of a rodent, having the same chisel-shaped form; they have, however, an addition in the shape of a keel, which runs along the back. The microscopist is perhaps the most curious and prying individual in the world, and does not suffer any object to escape his magnified inspection. Even the teeth of the sea-urchins have had to pay toll, and be subjected to the same severe scrutiny! In Fig. 83 we have a section of one of these teeth, whence it will be observed by those learned in such matters that there is a striking resemblance in the structure to

Fig. 83.

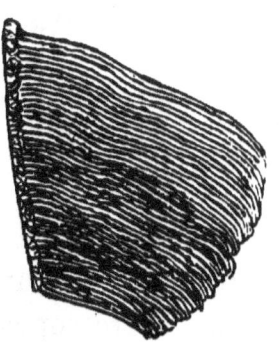

Section of Tooth.

that of the teeth of higher animals. The keel of these teeth, to which we have referred, is composed of rods of carbonate of lime, which lie oblique to the axis of the tooth. The chisel-shaped edge consists first of a series of triangular, calcareous plates, called "primary plates." These constitute a framework with which the other parts become connected. To these plates, at some distance from the base, are attached a series of lappet-shaped laminæ, to which are added reticulations of limy fibres, having a fan-shaped termination. Altogether, therefore, it will be seen that the structure of the teeth of sea-urchins is really very complex. In Fig. 84 we have a longi-

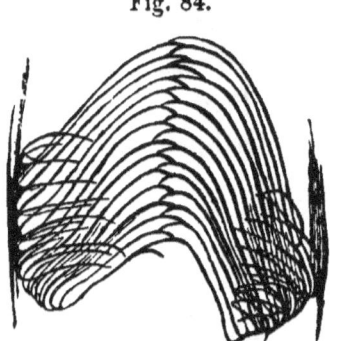

Fig. 84.

Longitudinal Section of Tooth.

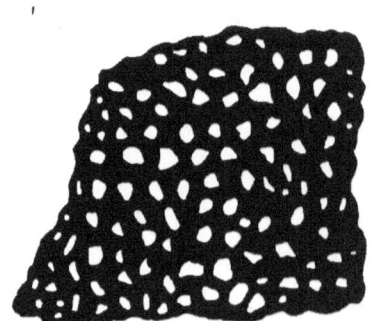

Fig. 85.

Portion of Shell of *Echinus lividus*, × 230.

tudinal section, showing the manner in which the minute plates of lime interlap each other.

The microscopical structure of the shell-case, or "test," of the sea-urchin is no less interesting. We have spoken about the number of pieces which are mosaicked together to form this test, and in Fig. 85

we give our readers an illustration of a magnified portion of one of these pieces, as it may be seen in the purple echinus (*Echinus lividus*) of our shores. Sections of the thorn-like spines of the same species form really beautiful objects for the microscope. Cross sections of the spines of some species look like exogenous wood, and even in those of the Purple Echinus this woody appearance is very striking.

Fig. 86.

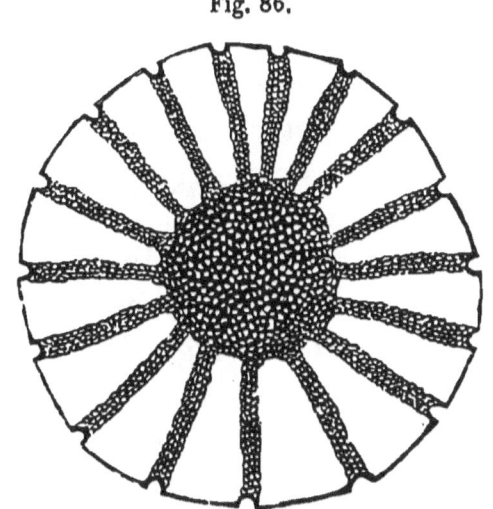

Transverse Section of Spine of *Echinus lividus*, × 60.

Just as exogenous wood has its annular rings, due to the successive deposition of woody tissue formed each year, so that the age of the tree may be known by merely counting them; so are the minute rings seen in the section of the spines of some echini evidences of the age of these animals, the lime having been deposited at successive times. The spines of the Purple Sea-urchin, however, are shed and reproduced annually, so that this concentric structure is not observable. But, as seen in Fig. 86, there are certain solid ribs and bands of open calcareous network, the latter coloured purple, which chequer the surface.

Whilst speaking of the spines of sea-urchins, we may notice certain minute and curious bodies which occur both on them and on the spines of some of the star-fishes, which were formerly supposed to be separate parasitic animals. They are called *Pedicellariæ*, and are now considered as simple appendages to the spines, although their true functions have not yet been clearly made out. Each of them consists of a thin stalk, formed of carbonate of lime, which is surmounted by a curious, pincer-like apparatus (Fig. 87). The whole is invested with the general animal membrane of the sea-urchin. The pincers are double, and are formed of a fine, calcareous net-work, resembling that of the shell. The edges of each limb of the pincers are serrated, and the whole structure is constantly engaged in a ludicrous snapping. Besides these peculiar objects for the microscope, obtainable from sea-urchins, we have others known as spicules, which occur in various parts of the body. In our most abundant species, the common

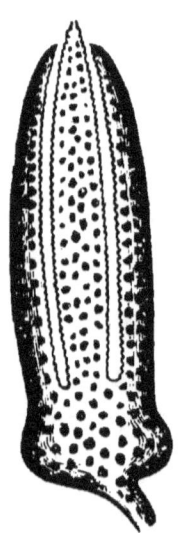

Fig. 87.

Pedicellaria, × 60.

egg-urchin (*Echinus sphæra*), these spicules are C-shaped, as shown in Fig. 88. The spicules of another species of sea-urchin found on our northern coasts (*Echinus drobrachiensis*) are very peculiar, having the appearance of bent thigh-bones (Fig. 89).

Fig. 88.  Fig. 89.

Spicules of *Echinus sphæra*.   Spicules of *Echinus drobrachiensis*.

The nervous system in the sea-urchins consists of a ring which encircles the gullet, and thence sends forth radiating branches to the various parts of the body. The intestine is twisted or convoluted. The interior of the shell and various parts is richly lined with cilia, which keep up a constant circulation, and distribute the fluids all over the body. Their higher organization is further shown by the fact that the sexes are separate, each possessing distinct reproductive organs. The young, both of the sea-urchins and the star-fish, do not resemble their parents in the slightest degree. Indeed, the fry of the former were esteemed a distinct genus of marine animals, and named *Pluteus*. Whilst the adults have a uniformly radiate, or star-shaped, structure, the young are bi-lateral; that is, have two equal sides. Singularly enough, the adult sea-urchin is developed only out of a *part* of the young " Pluteus."

Dredged up from the same depths as the Echinus, are specimens of a heart-shaped animal, covered with dark purple spines like the true sea-urchin. This is the *Spatangus*, which may readily be recognised from its shape, and its depressed height. Both the sea-urchins and the spatangus are sad gluttons, and may usually be found in the neighbourhood of oysters banks, on which they commit great depredations. The sea-urchins and the star-fish are connected by an intervening series, commenced by the spatangi on the one hand, and the " Cushion-stars " (*Clypeaster*, &c.) on the other. The latter are five-sided, and do not possess arms. They are peculiar, however, to warmer climates than ours.

In the true star-fish, of which we may take our common British species, the " Five-finger " (*Uraster rubens*, Fig. 90), as a familiar example, the skin which covers the upper surface, as seen in the illustration, has the power, in varying degrees, of secreting carbonate of lime, to strengthen it in the shape of spines, &c. On the under side, we find each arm deeply furrowed, and along the furrows are *four* rows of ambulacral, or sucking feet, like those described in the sea-urchin, and hydrostatically worked in a similar manner. When a star-fish has been turned over so as to bring the grooved surface of the arms uppermost, the student sees the mode in which these sucking feet operate. After a short time, one row after another begin to protrude, like so many white thread-worms, waving to and fro until they come into contact with some foreign body. To this they attach themselves by means of their suckers, and their discovery is an encouragement for hosts of other feet to bend over in the same

" Five Fingers."

direction, until they also have gained a foothold. Presently, when a sufficient number have been thrown out, an effort is made, and over goes the body of the star-fish! The presence of these grooves along the arms is one of the distinctive features of the true star-fishes. To see the star-fish glide, not crawl, over all kinds of uneven surfaces, being unarrested by sloping or even perpendicular rock-walls, one would never imagine that the only means they possessed of overcoming such difficulties was their hundreds of thread-like suckers. Their mouth is in the centre of the lower surface, but it has no teeth like the sea-urchin. And yet it is surprising what large-sized molluscs it manages to swallow, appearing to dissolve the shells by its strong gastric juice. The manner in which star-fish feed on oysters is very peculiar; they are the worst enemies of that favourite dainty; so much so that it is not long since a law existed, enacting that no fisherman should throw overboard a star-fish that had got entangled in his net. Of course, these animals have not the power of mechanically forcing open the solid shells of oysters, although the ancients thought they had. But they seem provided with some subtle poison which they instil into the oyster, the result being that the latter gets immediately benumbed, and yields up the ghost. The ravages which star-fish commit on oyster-banks are dreadful. But it has been found that the cuttle-fish is quite as fond of the star-fish, and by introducing them to their neighbourhood oyster-growers might realise a practical benefit. Many parts of the sea-bottom are literally carpeted by these star-fish, so that we may expect few chances for molluscs to survive under such circumstances. The anus of the star-fish is situated on the upper surface of the animal.

We have referred to the stomach of this creature, but should now add that this stomach is prolonged into each arm in the true star-fishes, thus forming another distinctive feature. In the "Brittle-stars" (*Ophiura*) it is confined to the body, and does not enter the arms at all. The nervous system consists of a ganglionated ring running round the mouth, and sending branches up each arm. The "Sun-star" (*Solaster papposa*) is another common British species, which may be readily known by its twelve arms or rays. They have only two rows of suckers in each furrow, but, like the Urasters, they are distinguished by having the back rounded or arched, the Asteroids being flat. The beauty of their skin is also noticeable, being usually of a red or a reddish-purple colour. The *Solaster* is abundant along all the coasts of Western Europe. There is a singular arrangement at the ends of each arm, in the shape of tentacular processes, and a so-called eye-speck, of a scarlet colour, which is protected by rows of spiny fans. So voracious is the sun-star, that he does not hesitate to devour the sea-urchin, spines and shell and all!

We now come to another familiar group of star-fish, whose peculiar custom of throwing off their arms in pieces when alarmed has earned for them the deserved name of "Brittle-star." It is of this species that Professor Edward Forbes speaks as follows:—"The common Brittle-star often congregates in great numbers on the edge of scallop banks, and I have seen a large dredge come up completely filled with them: a most curious sight; for when the dredge was emptied, the little creatures, writhing with the strangest contortions, crept about in all directions, often flinging their arms in broken pieces around them." Further on, in speaking of the "Lingthorn Star" (*Luidia fragilissima*), which is one of the largest of the tribe, he says:—"The first time that I took one of these creatures, I succeeded in placing it entire in my boat. Not having seen one before, and being ignorant of its suicidal powers, I spread it out on a rowing bench, the better to admire its form and colours. On attempting to remove it for preservation, to my horror and disappointment I found only an assemblage of detached members. My conservative endeavours were all neutralized by its destructive exertions, and the animal is now badly represented in my cabinet by a diskless arm, and an armless disk! Next time I went to dredge at the same spot I determined not to be cheated out of my specimen a second time. I carried with me a bucket of fresh water, for which the star-fishes evince a great antipathy. As I hoped, a *Luidia* soon came up in the dredge—a most gorgeous specimen. As the animal does not generally break up until it is raised to the surface of the sea, I carefully and anxiously plunged my bucket to a level with the dredge's mouth, and softly introduced the *Luidia* into fresh water. Whether the cold was too much for it, or the sight of the bucket too terrific, I do not know, but in a moment it began to dissolve its corporation, and I saw its limbs escaping through every mesh of the dredge. In my despair I seized the largest piece, and brought up the extremity of an arm with its terminal eye, the spinous eyelid of which opened and closed with something exceedingly like a wink of derision!" The true "Brittle-stars" are distinguished by having their central disk covered with a series of calcareous plates, in which is situated the stomach. We have already mentioned that the arms contain neither prolongation of the stomach, nor ambulacral or sucking-feet. The arms seem to be the special organs of locomotion, and these are endowed with great flexibility, and are able to twist and contort themselves in every possible position, and pull themselves along. These arms are defended by four rows of calcareous plates, one row on each side, one above and one below. All the internal organs are placed in the disk, except the nerves, which ramify up each arm. The *Ophiura* is a very short-lived species, and frequently goes by the distinctive name of "Sand-star." The true "Brittle-star" is *Ophiocoma*, which is much longer-lived when it has the opportunity of hiding up.

There are several British species of the last mentioned genus, among which *Ophiocoma rosula* is the prettiest, and perhaps commonest, although the "Granulate Brittle-star" (*Ophiocoma granulata*) is also very widely distributed. The latter lives in deep water, and crawls along the sea-bottom by means of its long arms. Mr. Fred. Kitton, of Norwich, has, we think, thrown some light on the means by which these animals are able to use their arms as means of locomotion, in a paper contributed to Hardwicke's "Science Gossip" in September, 1866.

Fig. 91.

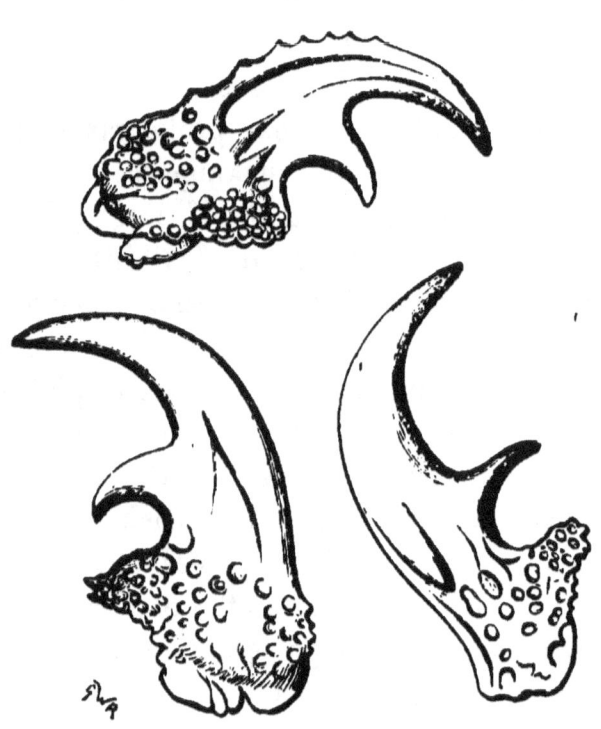

Claws from *Ophiocoma rosula*, × 150.

He found that whilst examining the remains of an arm of *O. rosula*, after maceration in caustic potash, a number of claw-shaped bodies, like those shown in Fig. 91, presented themselves. These claws had not previously been noticed by any naturalist. By the aid of the microscope, Mr. Kitton examined their position, in an arm with the spines and plates *in situ*, and found them attached to the lower margin of the side ray-plate, near the base of the last spine, as shown in Fig. 92. These claws have a cellular

Fig. 92.

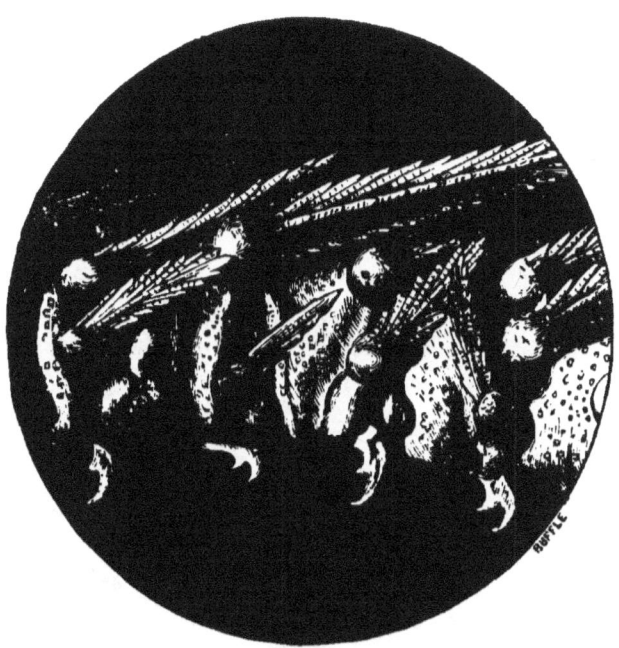

Portion of one of the rays of *Ophiocoma rosula*, showing the "claws" or "hooks" *in situ*, × 25.

burr on their lower portion, the remainder being smooth and glassy. The inner margin of each claw has a spur curving downwards, and Mr. Kitton was of opinion that they were useful in locomotion. Another species of "Brittle-star" is that which Professor Edward Forbes has named *Ophiocoma neglecta.* In Fig. 93 are seen two drawings of this creature, one of which is magnified, and the other showing it in its natural size. From the larger engraving the reader will obtain a good idea of the general appearance of the "Brittle-stars." This

Fig. 93.

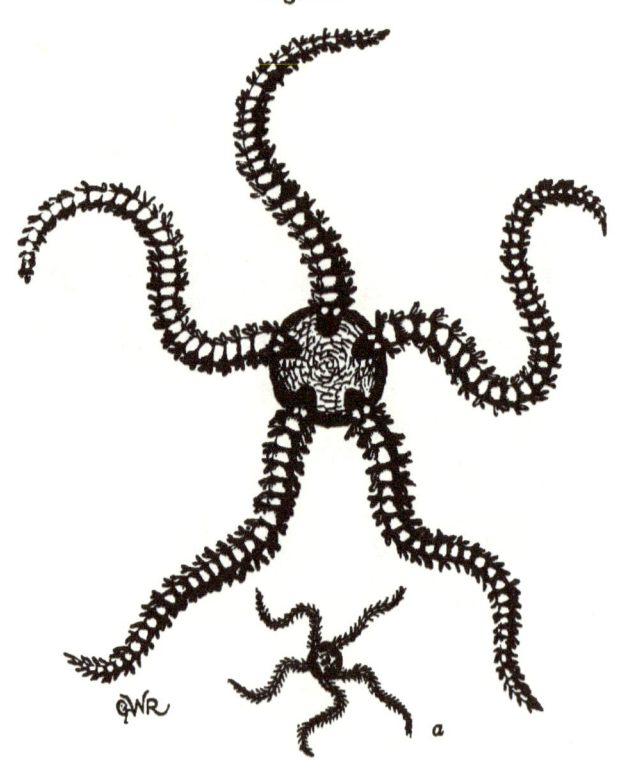

*Ophiocoma neglecta.* (*a.* natural size.)

pretty little species last mentioned never exceeds an inch in diameter. Major Holland mentions that just by the outlet of the drainage excavations at the base of East Cliff, at Hastings, it may be collected in hundreds. We have already referred to a sudden plunge in fresh water as being the best means of killing them, before they can mutilate themselves. At the place now referred to, a cluster of rocks is left bare at low water, and their surfaces contain numerous "pools," in which repose the mussels, &c., that have been torn from their moorings and separated from each other. Among the byssus of this shell-fish the little *Ophiocoma neglecta* may be found by scores. When dried by exposure to the air, after a cold water bath, they are indeed most beautiful objects for the cabinet. With the exception of a few other British localities, this species is not common. The same peculiarity of breaking off their arms characterises them everywhere. We may add that the Brittle-stars are no mean swimmers—an advantage they possess over their other brethren. The cod-fish is especially fond of this animal, and entire specimens may frequently be found in its stomach.

We proceed to give a brief notice to another member of this family, which connects the star-fishes with the ancient Encrinites. The latter are all but extinct, although the limestones of many of the Palæozoic rocks are crowded with their remains. The Carboniferous limestones of Derbyshire and Lancashire are especially so, as the polished marble of our mantel-pieces silently but certainly informs us. The "encrinital marble" of Derbyshire is almost wholly made up of the broken stems and joints of this old-world creature. One species of encrinite has recently been met with, during the deep-sea explorations, off the northern portion of the British Islands. But the object we would now draw attention to is known as the "Feather-star" (*Comatula rosacea*). It is not common, although we have seen it repeatedly brought in by the trawl fishermen. It has ten long arms, each of which is composed of joints formed of lime. These arms are feathered, as it were, along each side; hence the name of the animal. Singularly enough, when young, the feather-star is attached by a jointed stalk to the sea-bottom, and in this stage exactly resembles the encrinites. It is to be met with in the sea from Norway to the Mediterranean. When it reaches the adult state it separates from the stalk and swims away, progressing by alternate contractions and unfoldings of its long arms.

The sea-cucumbers (*Holothuriæ*) are nearly allied to the creatures we have been endeavouring to describe, in many respects. Off the Devonshire coast they are not uncommon, although they have not a very great northerly distribution. Were it not for the beautiful, feathery tentacles arranged round the head, they would be esteemed almost too ugly for notice. They have a knack of turning themselves almost inside out, when they present anything but an attractive appearance. They are more or less worm-shaped, and their tough skin is strengthened by the distribution through it of grains or spicules of carbonate of lime. Many of these form very attractive microscopical objects, as may be seen from Figs. 94 and 95, the anchor-

Fig. 94.

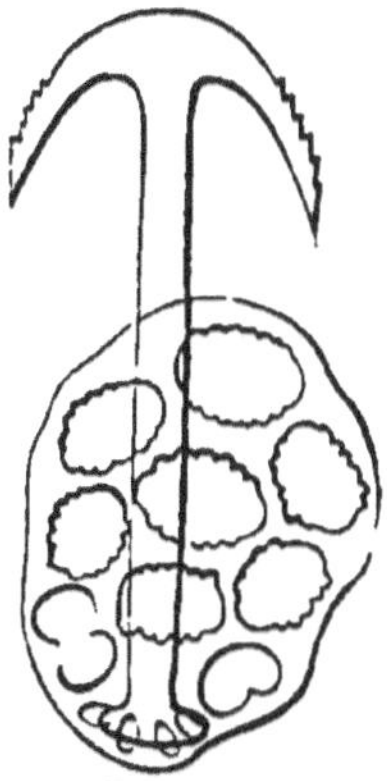

Fig. 95.

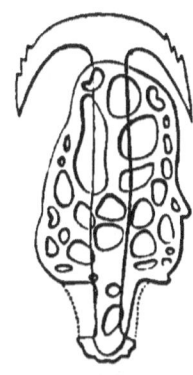

Anchor and Plate of *Synapta inhærens*.

Anchor and Plate of *Synapta digitata*.

shaped spicules being characteristic of one genus, *Synapta*. Two other species occur in British seas, one of them as far north as the Outer Hebrides—*Synapta Gallienii*. This is also to be met with off the Channel Islands. The spicules of another species, also British, called *Synapta Buskii* (Fig. 96), are very remarkable in their shape. Foreign species of the same class of marine animals are much prized for the graceful and delicate beauty of the spicules, and

Fig. 96.

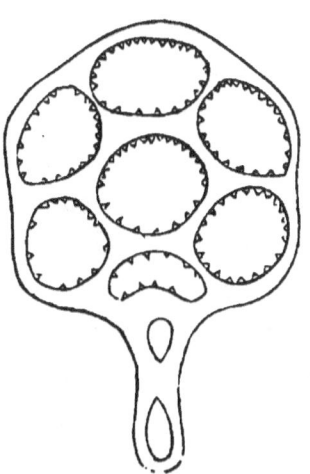

Plate of *Synapta Buskii*.

most of them may be obtained from any first-class optician. As examples of these we give the forms of plates seen in Figs. 97 and 98, from genera which are closely allied to the *Synapta*. The Holothuriæ go by the popular name of "sea-cucumbers," on account of their rude resemblance, when distended, to the seed pods of that well-known plant. They possess sucking, or ambulacral feet, as do the starfishes and sea-urchins, although not to the same degree. The mouth is situated at one end of the

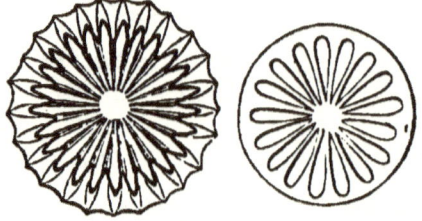

Wheels of *Myriotrochus Rinkii*.    Wheel of *Chirodota violacea*.

body—that where the feathery tentacles are—and the arms at the other. Our British species are usually met with chiefly in deep water. In the Indian Ocean these animals attain a larger size, and regular fisheries are established, because, when dry, they are greatly in demand among the Chinese, with whom it is known as "Trepang." Its taste is said to resemble that of the lobster.

Let any one who is anxious to know more about the objects treated on in this chapter get Professor Forbes' "Monograph of the British Star-fishes." He will there find all our native species described in a manner at once enthusiastic and humorous, and if he does not laugh at the ludicrous " tail-pieces " in which the wayward fancy of the Professor indulged, we do not envy him his grim nature. For, if anything can soften a man's heart, and keep it green, it is the study of natural history in its various departments. Perhaps in no other branch of human learning is it so possible to realise the poet's well known line, and

"Look through Nature, up to Nature's God!"

## XI.

#### HALF AN HOUR WITH SHELL-FISH (UNIVALVES).

PERHAPS no objects are so eagerly sought after, or so much admired, at the sea-side, as shells. They are pretty enough to be thought worthy of transference, for even the commonest has an interest transcending that of other creatures. How was it possible for animals so lowly organised, with no evident architectural means for the purpose, to build up mechanically regular dwelling-places like these? Science teaches us that beneath the most familiar appearances there often lurk lessons of profoundest wisdom. It is only ignorance that sneers at a pursuit because it deals with commonplace objects. Nay, the scientific man is aware that the more he enters into the structural details of the lowliest creature, the more numerous are the practical lessons he is likely to learn!

The law which regulates even such an apparently trivial matter as the mode in which the shells of univalves twist or turn, is as mathematically true as the conic sections we find entering into the orbits of planets and comets. Mr. Moseley has shown that the size of the whorls, and the distance between contiguous whorls, in such shells as the common Wentle-trap (*Turritella communis*) of our shores, follow a geometrical progression. The spiral formed is the logarithmic, of which it is a property that it is everywhere the same geometrical curvature, and is the only curve, except the circle, which possesses this property. Following this law, the animal winds its dwelling in a uniform direction through the space round its axis. We cannot forbear quoting Mr. Moseley's own remarks on this subject, which will be found in a paper contributed to the "Philosophical Transactions" as far back as 1838: "There is traced in this shell, the application of properties of a geometrical curve to a mechanical purpose, by Him who metes the dimensions of space, and stretches out the forms of matter according to the rules of a perfect geometry!" There is another circumstance in connection with univalve shells we would mention. It is evident that in aquatic mollusca the shell must not only be a habitation for the animal, but a float. This it becomes through the portion of the narrower extremity of the shell being left unoccupied. But in order to preserve its buoyancy, and enable the animal to ascend and descend the water at will, it is necessary that the increase in the capacity of its float should bear a constant ratio to the corresponding increase of its body. This ratio always assigns a greater amount to the former than to the latter. It is in accordance with the geometrical character of the form assumed that the capacity of the shell and the dimensions of the animal do increase in a constant ratio, causing the whole bulk of the animal to bear a relation of constantly increasing inequality to the whole capacity of the shell. The subject is one of profoundest interest, not only to naturalists, but also to mathematicians; and, although it is next to impossible for us to place it before our non-mathematical readers in a more simplified form, enough has been said to show what important laws underlie such seemingly trivial things as the shape and size of a univalve shell to the mollusc that inhabits it. To quote Mr. Moseley's own words again : "God hath bestowed upon this humble architect the practical skill of a learned mathematician!"

We have purposely devoted the present chapter to "Univalves," because the marine mollusca, even of our British seas, are very numerous. It is next to impossible for the sea-side visitor to take a walk along the beach for any distance without seeing the dead shells, both of bivalves and univalves, lying about. Their size ranges from that of the large red whelk, to the minute *Rissoas* and *Kellias* that are only to be found by turning over the stones at low water, and, even then, only by a sharp pair of eyes. By the term "univalves" is usually meant all those shells which are composed of one piece, as the periwinkle, for instance. But it is found to be impossible to draw a hard and fast line in natural history anywhere, and it is equally so here. Many of the shells now included under this general term are in reality composed of *many* pieces, such as the

*Chitons;* whilst others, as the sea-slugs, have no shell at all. These all belong to that order called *Gasteropoda*, or "belly-creepers," in allusion to their mode of progression being like that of the common land-snail.

We purpose, however, drawing attention first to certain marine animals whose organisation is considerably higher than those just named. They are included in an order—once very numerous—called *Cephalopoda*, or "head-footed," on account of the long arms being arranged round the head. A good deal of interest has lately been excited in this class of animals, by the introduction of one of them, the "Cuttle-fish," in the aquarium of the Crystal Palace. Its intense ugliness and seeming ferocity has earned for it the name of the "Sea Devil!" A good idea of its general appearance may be obtained from Fig. 99. Perhaps it will be as well, before entering farther into the details of the structure of this and other nearly allied animals, if we devote a short space to a consideration of the *general* characters of the family to which they belong.

First of all we may remark that the *Cephalopoda* have been in existence longer than any other class of shell-fish, or mollusca, except the "Lamp-shells" (*Brachiopoda*). They date from the early Silurian age, and their remains are found more or less crowding the limestones of every geological period since then. This early group, however, is more nearly allied to the nautilus of the Indian Ocean, than to our

British cuttle-fish. In the Lias formation we find representatives of the modern group beginning to get the upper-hand, and this dominancy continued until the Nautilus family dwindled down to one or two species. In the chalk formation there occur an abundance of common, fossils which go by the popular name of "thunder-bolts." Ignorance

Fig. 99.

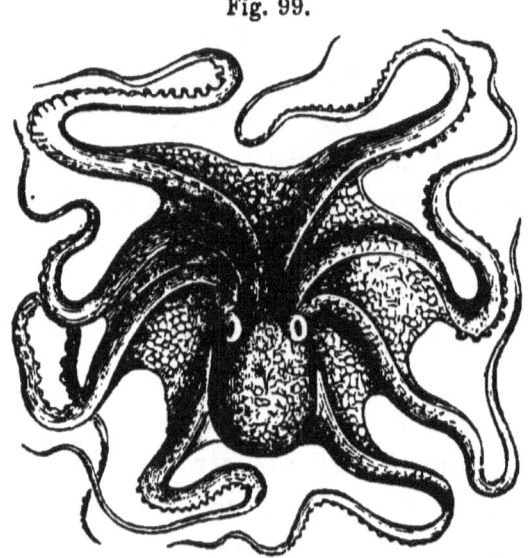

Cuttle-fish, or *Octopus*.

ascribes their origin to thunder-storms, all England over. These objects, however, are nothing more or less than the terminal bones of an extinct genus of cuttle-fish, which was very abundant during the Secondary age, but which is now extinct, and represented only by the modern cuttle-fish, whose bone (*Sepiostaire*) may be also found in some abundance after a storm, and is made to do duty for

HALF AN HOUR WITH SHELL-FISH. 185

tooth-powder! All the members of this family, recent and extinct, are carnivorous. Their long arms, as shown in Fig. 99, are formed by a splitting up of the margin round the head into eight parts, popularly termed "feet;" hence the name of the animal, *Octopus*—"eight-footed." By means of these arms or feet (for they are made to do duty for both) the cuttle-fish can crawl along the sea-bottom, head downwards, and search there for its prey. When observed with the arms less actively occupied,

Fig. 100.

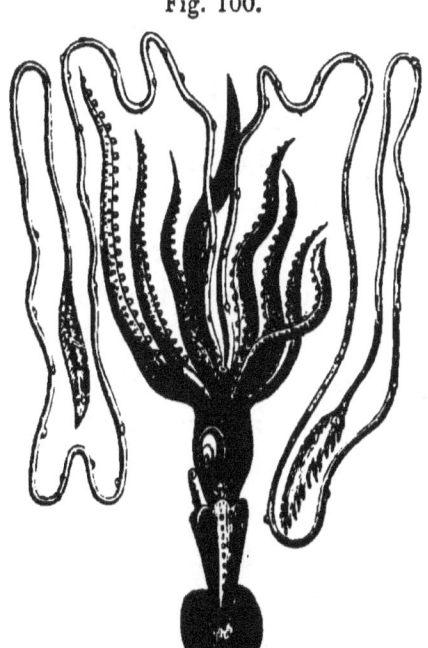

*Loligopsis.*

it will be noticed that the body indicates something like proportionate moulding (Fig. 100, *Loligopsis*).

There is the head, with eyes, mouth, &c., and the posterior part, containing the internal organs. The mouth is very peculiar for its horny jaws, which are hardened by carbonate of lime diffused through the tissues, and are not unlike those of a parrot in appearance. The tongue, also, is no less striking, being armed with recurved spines, so that the mechanism for getting rid of prey is pretty perfect. The mouth leads into an internal muscular cavity, for the further trituration of the food. Not less curious are the eyes of the cuttle-fish, which have long been a puzzle to naturalists and opticians, although they seem to approach, in structure, the "Coddrington lens" more than anything else. Sir David Brewster and other learned men have devoted their attention specially to the optical principles on which the eyes of this creature are based. Another curious and remarkable contrivance—for this animal is full of singular adaptations—is the means of respiration and progression. Both these important functions are achieved by a very simple method. Just below the neck of the cuttle-fish, outside, may be noticed two slits, leading into what are called the "branchial chambers;" that is, the gill- or breathing-chambers, corresponding to the lungs of the higher animals. In the ordinary cuttle-fish there are placed two gills; in the Nautilus family four. The sea-water is admitted by the external apertures to these gills, and supplies them with the air that happens to be mechanically mixed up with it. After it has done its work in this respect, it is forced by muscular action into a siphon, formed by a folding of the external leathery coat, and out again. The water thus forced outwards becomes a means of locomotion, and forces the animal backwards. Hence it is that the cuttle-fish always swims backwards, locomotion and respiration going on at the same time, and by the same means.

We have referred to the comparatively high position which the cuttle-fish holds among the mollusca. In many respects, it seems to connect them with the vertebrata, not only in its complex eyes, but in its internal bone, which answers to a vertebrate structure, and in its nervous structure. That part of the latter placed near the head is termed the "cerebral ganglion," and this is protected by a cartilage that seems to foreshadow the skull in the true vertebrate animals. The sexes of the cuttle-fish are distinct, and the means of reproduction very curious. First, one of the arms of the male becomes seemingly stunted, so as to form a bladder-like appearance. This eventually bursts, and then the arm shoots out much longer than the rest, terminating in a peculiar oval plate. It is the latter, and that alone, which seems to have the function of transmitting the sperm-cells to the female cuttle-fish. On looking at the illustration, it will be observed that each arm is covered with suckers. These form most formidable aids to the animal's carnivorous tastes, and when an arm is once applied, and the sucker fixed, it is easier to tear the part off than to detach the sucker. Each sucker appears to be under the will and control of the animal, and is formed on the principle of a piston and cavity. When the sucker is applied, the piston is withdrawn, and thus an air-tight adherence is produced. The common sepia (*Sepia officinalis*) has no fewer than nine hundred of these distinct air-pumps or suckers.

The Calamaries and Squids—both of which occur in British seas—are distinguished from the "Poulpe" or *Octopus*, by having ten arms, instead of eight. These animals are found principally in the open sea, to which habit of life they are well adapted by the lateral fins on each side the neck, by means of which they are assisted in rapid swimming. Their shell is internal, and after death, is not unfrequently found cast up on the beach. The internal bone of the sepia is that commonly used in the manufacture of tooth-powder. It is crystalline—a structure which is not absolutely destroyed by the severest crushing. Under the microscope, with polarizing apparatus, it forms a most beautiful object. They are the eggs of this common species which may often be met with among heaps of cast-up seaweeds. Among the fishermen they go by the name of "Sea-grapes"—a not inappropriate term, if we go by their general appearance. In Fig. 101 we have an illustration of these cuttle-fish eggs, showing the young just emerging. The latter coolly enter on their existence much in the same shape as their parents, and immediately fall to their carnivorous habits. We have omitted to mention that curious means possessed by cuttle-fishes, of emitting a cloud of so-called "ink," by means of which they can muddy the water and conceal themselves. The fossil species seem to have also been provided with it, for it has been found in a fossil state, so well preserved through the millions of years that had elapsed since it was secreted, that

Fig. 101.

"Sea-grapes," or Eggs of Cuttle-fish.

it was used for sketching the animal's portrait. The bone of the common squid (*Sepiola atlantica*) is very abundant on our shores. It has a horny appearance, and in shape is not unlike the spatulate leaf of a plant. It is, however, very small, as the animal to which it belonged was not above two inches in length. Another common "Cuttle-bone" to be met with is that of the calamary (*Loligo vulgaris*), or "Sea-pen," about six inches long, and not unlike a quill-pen in appearance, hence its name.

The *Pteropoda* are oceanic mollusca, which take their name of "wing-footed" (as the above word literally means) from the fin-like expanses about the head, by means of which they swim. They are found chiefly in the open seas, especially in those of the north, in immense numbers, the water being perfectly thick with them. There they furnish the principal food of the whale. Occasionally, however, odd individuals of one genus, *Hyalea*, are cast on our shores, but their small size and glassy textures conceal them from general observation.

The next class of univalve shell-fish, however, more than makes up for this scantiness. Indeed, it is that to which the name of univalve most appropriately belongs, although, as we have already remarked, it contains many species which have no shells at all, and others whose shell is composed of many parts. As a rule, however, the shell is composed of a single piece, often beautifully ornamented in colour, and equally elegant in shape. The chief distinction of the group is the great development of the so-called foot, which forms a broad, flat disk, with which the animals creep about. Many species have what is called an *operculum* attached to it—that is, a plate composed of the same substance as the shell, and so fixed that, when the mollusc has withdrawn itself into its shell, it can close the aperture by means of this contrivance. It is on account of this class of molluscs creeping about on their broad foot that they go by the name of *Gasteropoda*, or "belly-footed." In all the species, the head is distinct, and usually surmounted by two feelers or tentacles, and close by are two eyes, generally placed on stalks. Within the mouth is the "lingual ribbon," a strap-shaped organ crowded with teeth, which works to and fro, and thus enables the creature to bore holes even through the solid shells of bivalves. The siliceous teeth and ribbon are differently shaped in different species, and all have long been favourite objects with microscopists. The stomach of many species is provided with a peculiar set of calcareous plates, used in the trituration of food. The intestine is usually well-developed and very long, terminating in a distinct aperture, called the *anus*. The liver, also, is very large considering the size of the animal, and seems to be a most important organ. The heart is provided with two chambers, arterial and venous.

As regards the arrangements by which respiration is carried on in the *Gasteropoda*, a good deal of diversity exists. It may be effected in three different ways; first, by exposing the blood simply to the action of the air contained in the water; second, by special breathing organs in the form of outward processes of the skin, exposed to view on the back or sides of the animal, as in the common *Doris*; or third, by breathing organs, as feathery gills, contained in a chamber improvised by a simple folding or doubling of the mantle. To the latter contrivance the water is usually admitted by a tube or siphon, the effete, or exhausted water, being expelled by another tube, carrying away the fæces, or excrements, of the animal away with it. The young of all the gasteropods, as a rule, are provided with an embryonic shell, and swim freely about by means of ciliated lobes placed near the head, which give to them the appearance of the pteropods. As the latter are among the oldest known shell-fish, it is not improbable that the gasteropods were derived through them, and still exhibit their descent in their embryonic condition.

We have already dwelt on the geometrically designed structure of a univalve shell. The normal plan is realized, perhaps, most simply in the Common Limpet, (*Patella vulgata*, Fig. 102), where it consists of a hollow cone, having the apex a little on one side. The *spiral* form, however, is the commonest; and this is best typified in the common wentle-trap (*Turritella communis*). The last and largest of the whorls, when there are several, is called the "body-whorl." A simple means of identifying the

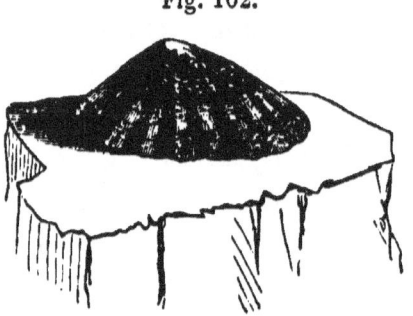

Fig. 102.

Limpet (*Patella vulgata*).

carnivorous univalves from the herbivorous class exists in the shape of the mouth of the "body-whorl." When it is round or "entire," as in the wentle-trap, it is usually herbivorous; when notched, or prolonged into a canal, as in the Murex, it is carnivorous.

It will be as well to devote a few remarks to certain molluscs which, although they have no shells, are classed as gasteropods. They may be found clinging to or lying under rocks and stones at low water; and many of them compensate for their lack of elegant shells by their brilliant colours. On account of the way in which the gills are exposed, they are called *nudibranchs*, or "naked-gilled" molluscs. Popularly they go by the names of "sea-lemons," "sea-slugs," "sea-hares," &c. In fact, we may regard them as occupying a similar position in the marine world to that which the common black and yellow garden slugs do on land. Singularly enough, the nudibranch molluscs have an embryonic shell when young, which they lose as they approach the adult condition—a fact which throws some light on their descent, and indicates that they may be derived from ancestors which possessed a shell, and were true univalves. The gills, or *branchiæ*, are arranged in tufts along the back and sides, hence the name of the order. The nervous system is very highly developed, so much so that some naturalists regard them as holding the highest position among the gasteropods. This is a significant circumstance, taken into consideration with their possession of an embryonic shell, and certainly points in the direction of their having been evolved from simpler shell-bearing ancestors.

A common example of this group is the "Sea-hare" (*Aplysia*), so called on account of the tentacles and head resembling the head and ears of a couching hare. The animal is about three inches in length, and is generally of a dark olive colour, varying in tints and shades of other colours. It is remarkable for the power it possesses of exuding a bright purple fluid when dropped into the fresh sea-water of the bell-glass, causing the whole to assume the appearance of port wine. It was formerly supposed that this fluid would take off the hair, a notion which gave the name of *depilans* to a common species. The "Sea-hare" is noted for its peculiar gastric arrangements, consisting of three stomachs, like those of a ruminant, the middle one of which acts as a gizzard, and is armed with horny plates for grinding down the coarser sea-weeds on which it feeds. Nearly allied to the "Sea-hare" is the "Sea-lemon" (*Doris*), which abounds generally on the perpendicular faces of rocks, and averages two or three inches in length. Its popular name is derived from its appearance, resembling the half of a cut emon—a likeness borne out by the yellow colour and the warty surface. The gills, or *branchiæ*, are feathery, and eight in number, the whole being expanded when the animal is in the water, like the petals of a beautiful flower. These are placed towards the hinder part of the body. Another not uncommon species of nudibranch, to be found under stones, &c., is the *Æolis*, by far the most beautiful of all. The gills are placed as a series of rows of fibres, transversely across the back (Fig. 103), and are of

Fig. 103.

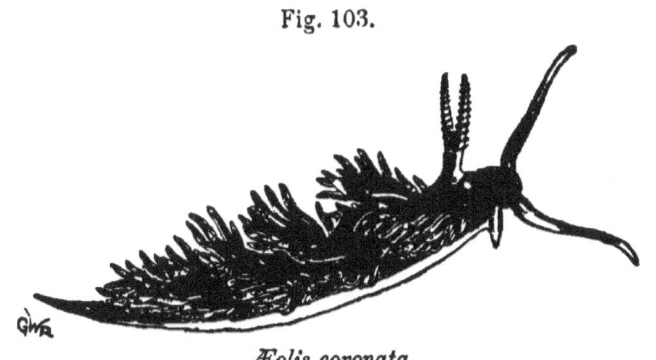

*Æolis coronata.*

the richest crimson and blue colours, especially noticeable when the creature is placed in an aquarium. The body is long and slender, tapering to a fine point behind. The combined effect of the brilliantly contrasted colours, and of the pellucid gill-fibres, is very charming; so that there is little wonder this animal should be such a great favourite with naturalists. But innocently lovely though it seems, it is a deadly foe to the sea-anemones, attacking and devouring them as a hungry carnivorous animal would a lamb. Most of the nudibranchs spawn early in the year, generally before May; and their egg-ribbons form very interesting objects. That of the "Sea-lemon" is like a pasty ribbon, rolled up loosely.

The Æolis has a frilled scroll, arranged spirally. When minutely examined these ribbons are seen to consist of rows of eggs, imbedded in a clear jelly-looking substance. The Æolis brings forth an enormous number of these eggs, frequently not less than a quarter of a million in a year. Space forbids us noticing other than the typical and commonest of the nudibranch mollusca, there being a great number living even in our British seas.

As regards the true univalves, it is necessary to look keenly out for specimens; for our English species do not equal in size those of tropical seas. Most of them are very minute, and only to be found after much searching under stones, in mud, among sea-weeds, &c. But the morning after a storm ought never to be missed being turned to advantage, for that is the only opportunity of obtaining the deeper water species, except the student has the opportunity of dredging, or manages to arrange with the trawl-fishers to save him those they scrape up from the deep sea-bottom. On the rocks and stones the commonest objects are the limpets and the periwinkles. The former we have already referred to, and its appearance is undoubtedly well known to the majority of our readers. It is seen to the best advantage when placed in the aquarium; although, unfortunately, it does not live long there, for some cause or another. Only there will you have a chance of observing its head and tentacles, for it is a very sensitive and cautious animal. The "tooth-ribbon" of the limpet has long been a favourite object with microscopists, as, when mounted, it shows the numerous rows of teeth, amounting to more than two thousand in number. The powerful manner with which the limpet adheres to rocks and stones has been proverbial for ages. Reaumur found that a weight of nearly thirty pounds was required to detach a single individual from its hold. This wonderful power of adherence is brought about mainly by suction, assisted by a very strong natural glue, which the animal has the means of secreting. We have various species of limpet in our native seas. Among others may be noticed *Patella pellucida*, obtained from deeper water, and often to be found adhering to the roots of the larger sea-weeds when these have been cast up. It has, as its specific name implies, a semi-pellucid shell, ornamented by blue lines which radiate from the apex to the margin. *Patella athletica*, or "Horse-limpet," is larger, and has bold spiny ribs projecting down its sides. It is not an uncommon shell. Nearly allied to the above is the little *Acmea*—a shell most common on our northern shores. When fresh, it is beautifully mottled with chestnut and white. It is, however, only about half an inch in length.

The Limpet family includes a good many allied genera, among which the *Chitons* are perhaps the most remarkable (Fig. 104). Their shells are composed of a number of plates, slightly overlapping each other, so that it curls up when the animal has been extracted from it. We have several species, all of which more or less affect the same habits, and are to be found under stones at low water. The largest is *Chiton ruber*, and the commonest *Chiton cinereus*, an ashen, grey-coloured shell, often mottled with yellow or chocolate. The "Key-hole Limpets" (*Fissurella*) take their name from their peculiar appearance, which is as if the common limpet had had its apex cut off so as to leave an aperture resembling a key-hole. This hole is used by the animal for discharging the effete and used-up sea-water. The "Notched Limpets" (*Emarginula*, Fig. 105) have, as their name implies, a small vertical notch cut in the basal portion of the shell, Fig. 105. These are, perhaps, the most elegant of the limpets, the white, finely-ribbed shell having the apex gently curved over. The gill-plumes are arranged on each side the animal's body.

Fig. 104.

*Chiton marmoreum.*

Fig. 105.

*Emarginula reticulata.*

Fig. 106.

*Trochus zizyphinus.*

Next we come to the "Topshells," most of which are shore-loving species, and deservedly rank among the most beautiful of our native mollusca. *Trochus zizy-*

*phinus* is a common species, and may be identified by its reddish zig-zag lines, Fig. 106. The foot of this mollusc is very peculiar, moving one half at a time. This feature, however, can only be observed when it is placed in an aquarium. In *Trochus cinereus* the top or apex of the shell is usually worn down very much, as if it had been dissolved away. It has markings very much like those of the previously mentioned species, but may be identified by its smaller size and eroded top. *Trochus majus* is noticeable for its large umbilicus— the perforation to be seen at the base of the shell, in the centre. The outside of this species has each whorl sharply ridged. All the "Top-shells" have opercula, or little doors, by means of which they can close the apertures or mouths of their shells. This is a common feature among the herbivorous univalves. The round mouths of all the "Top-shells" indicate that they belong to this class.

In the "Pheasant-shell" (*Phasianella*) the foot is actually divided into two halves, so that it can progress one half at a time. So far, therefore, it is allied to the "Top-shells." It is a very small mollusc, but a most elegant shell, delicately mottled with red and yellow zig-zag lines or blotches, and having a porcelain appearance, which renders its identification easy. Its entire length rarely exceeds a quarter of an inch. Of the true periwinkles (*Littorina littorea*) we have two varieties; one a large, dark, slate-coloured individual, and the other a bright, almost canary yellow. Both these are too well-known to need any verbal description. The *Nassas*, Fig. 107, or "Dog Whelks," are common British shells, and of these we have two species not difficult to meet with, *incrassata* and *reticulata*. The former has a long spire, and a thick lip to the mouth, whence its name. The latter may be easily identified, being much larger than the preceding, and having its external surface crossed with reticulated lines. The "Pelican's-foot" shell is one possessing greater interest. In this species (*Aporrhais pespelicani*) the lip of the shell is expanded, and then divided into claw-like processes, the whole greatly resembling the webbed foot of a water-fowl. The young undergoes a great many changes before it arrives at maturity. In its earliest condition there are no signs of an expanded lip, so that in this stage it bears little or no resemblance to its parent. Another not uncommon shell, especially on our southern coasts, is the little European cowry (*Cyprea Europea*). It is, perhaps, the most lovely of all our native shells, its delicate warm pink and chocolate blotches enhancing the transverse furrows which sweep across the shell, and gently curve round each end, Fig. 108. The mantle is so formed that it can invest the whole of the shell. It is a beautiful little creature for the aquarium, as the bright colours of the fleshy parts,

Fig. 107.

*Nassa reticulata.*

when protruded, are as pleasing, or more so, as the shell itself.

The "Purple-shell" (*Purpura lapillus*, Fig. 109) is nearly as abundant in every rockpool as the periwinkle. Along the southern coasts it is found of a white colour, with dark brown bands running up the centre of every whorl. It is a very stout, strong shell, and alters in its colour with age. In the northern seas, however, it would seem as if the pure white-grounded and brown-banded variety was much scarcer than farther south. The older specimens have the inner surface of the lip tinged with a rich, rosy purple. It takes its name from its power of exuding a purple dye, and it is believed to be one of the species that furnished the ancient Tyrian purple. The egg-cases of this shell may be found in abundance under ledges of rock, where, as Mr. Gosse remarks, they resemble "Nine-pins in shape, set on their ends in close contact with each other, and varying in numbers from three or four to a hundred or upwards in a group. Some of them are tinged with purple at the tips, and while sometimes you find them closed, and full of a yellow, creamy substance, at others they are open at the top and empty." The tongue

Fig. 108.

*Cyyrea Europea.*

Fig. 109.

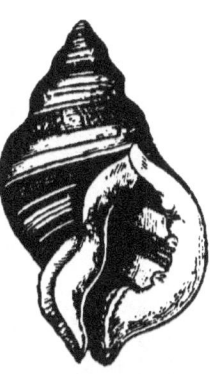

*Purpura lapillus.*

and teeth of the *Purpura* furnish good microscopic objects.

Underneath the stones and in the rock-pools there occur in abundance a minute shell, gracefully spiral, called *Rissoa*, of which there are several species, one of which is to be met with in brackish water. The *Naticas* are much larger shells, one species (*N. monilifera*, Fig. 110) exceeding the periwinkle in size. The surface of its whorls is mottled with pretty chocolate markings, but when alive the shell is almost entirely covered with the mantle. *Cerithium* resembles the *Turritella* in its elongated form, but is much more prettily ornamented with wavy, vertical ridges. Both these shells are very common on all our British shores. Not unfrequently there may be seen a little shell, whose name of "Tusk," or "tooth-shell," easily leads to its identification, for it exactly resembles a miniature tusk of an elephant, or the canine teeth of a rodent. This is the *Dentalium*, Fig. 111, and it belongs to the gasteropods, having all the principal features of that family. The *Cœcum* is a shell allied to it, which seems as if the *Dentalium* had been broken in halves, and the end plugged up. When empty, the *Dentalium* is seen to be open at each end.

Fig. 110.

*Natica monilifera.*

Fig. 111.

*Dentalium.*

And now we conclude our brief notice of the commoner British univalves by a reference to a species already known to all as the "White Whelk" (*Buccinum undatum*, Fig. 112.) It is often sold in our fish markets for food, as is also the "Red Whelk" (*Fusus antiquus*). Its shell may easily be identified from the deep furrows which run vertically up each whorl. This mollusc deposits its eggs in bags or

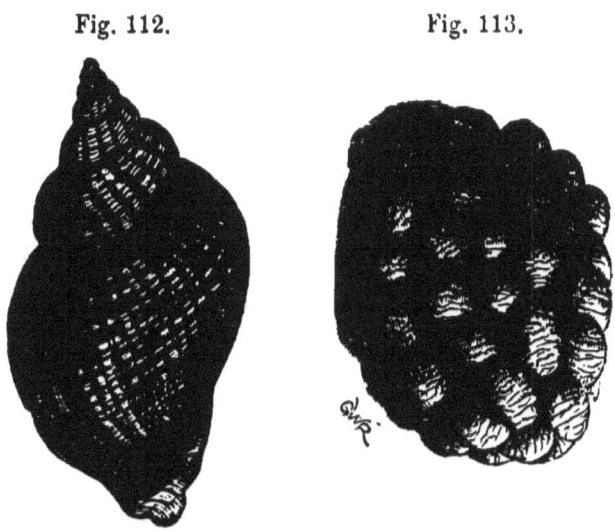

Fig. 112.   Fig. 113.

*Buccinum undatum.*   Egg-cases of *Buccinum.*

cases, the whole of which are grouped together. These empty egg-cases may frequently be picked up on the beach, where they exactly resemble a large bunch of hops, Fig. 113. The "Red Whelk" (*Fusus antiquus*) is dredged up further out at sea, and is much larger than the *Buccinum*. Its surface is smooth, and of an iron-red colour, whence its name. It is a very elegantly formed shell, and often kept for its shape. Occasionally, but rarely, specimens are found having the whorls turned the wrong way. This is a freak not limited to the *Fusus*, but met with rarely in all univalve shells. What is very singular, however, is that the earliest forms of the "Red Whelk," which occurs abundantly in the Suffolk Crag deposits in a fossil state, had all this sinistral or wrong twist, and hence they go by the name of *Fusus contrarius*. Space does not permit us to dwell at further length on our native univalves, but those who wish to enter on their study, as well as that of the bivalves, cannot do better than get the exhaustive work of Mr. Gwyn Jeffrys on British conchology, where every species known to inhabit English seas is fully described, both anatomically and conchologically.

## XII.

### HALF AN HOUR WITH SHELL-FISH (BIVALVES).

THE enormous fertility of marine mollusca can only be understood when we are thoroughly acquainted with the claims made upon them. They are caught in hundreds of millions every year, as cockles, mussels, oysters, &c., to be consumed by man. On many parts of our coasts, the mussel-beds are worked for the purpose of manuring the half-barren lands, and thousands of cartloads are carried off for this purpose. The bivalves, especially, furnish the principal food of the carnivorous univalve molluscs, and their perforated shells, thrown ashore, only too surely indicate the end that overtook them. The star-fishes fill their greedy maws with these dainties; fishes of many species find in them their staple food. And yet, in spite of these immense demands and ravages, the ocean bed is being covered in many places with calcareous deposits formed by the accumulation of dead shells, &c. The supply is much greater than the demand, and the excess is being utilised in laying the probable foundations for future continents.

This remark suggests to us the work done by certain lowly-organised molluscs in forming the actual solid land on which we live. In Derbyshire,

Warwickshire, Staffordshire, Yorkshire, Lancashire, and various other localities, you may see the limestones, hundreds of feet in thickness, belonging to the Silurian and Carboniferous formations, crowded, nay, actually made up with the remains of fossil shells. You examine these more minutely and find that they belong to a class which, although still living, seems to be gradually verging towards extinction. At least it occupies nothing like the cosmopolitan distribution and abundance it enjoyed in the earlier seas of the globe. This class goes by the name of *Brachiopoda*, or "arm-footed," on account of a certain internal structure to which we will presently call attention. We have two species existing in British seas, but they are not common, and only found at great depths. Until very lately their occurrence was most rare, and a specimen was worth considerable money value. Since deeper sea dredging became popular, and marine naturalists more numerous, these shells have turned up in greater abundance, so that they are not so rare, even in our smaller museums, as they formerly were. These species are *Terebratula caput serpentis*, commonly called the "Snake-head" Terebratula, and the *Crania norvegica*. The former is a delicate, finely striated shell, of a greyish-white colour, and about half an inch in length. Perhaps this is the oldest species of mollusc in existence, for our best Palæontologist, Mr. Davidson, believes it to be identical with a fossil species met with in the chalk formation. If so, then it must have had a continuous existence since that distant epoch—a period of time that is inconceivable, and that cannot be reckoned in years. The latter mollusc (*Crania*) takes its generic name from the supposed resemblance of the upper valve to a helmet. It is peculiar to our northern seas, as its specific name implies, and is not uncommonly met with off the shores of Scotland, during dredging operations. The *Crania*, as a rule, are found parasitically attached to other objects.

Although the brachiopods are classed among the bivalves, they really possess a nearer affinity to the "Sea-mats," or *Polyzoa*. A common name for them as a group is that of "Lamp-shells," on account of the resemblance of the closed valves to an antique lamp. The ventral valve is generally the larger, and the beak is perforated. Out of this perforation, in the living animals, there passes a kind of plug, or peduncle, the end of which attaches itself to stones, &c., and thus anchors the animal and its shell in safety. As far back as we can go in geological time, we find the "Lamp-shells" with perforated beaks. The interior of the shell is occupied with two long, coiled-up processes called "arms," which can be uncoiled and used for obtaining food. They also form the means by which the creature can breathe or respire. The interior shows the mouth, which is situated at the base of these arms; gullet, stomach, and liver. As is frequently the case with marine organism, although the adult animal is stationary, the embryo is a free-swimming creature, moving about by means of cilia.

The true bivalve mollusca are distinguished by having three pairs of nerve-cords, or ganglia, and a distinct heart, which has two chambers. The scientific name given to this class of *Lamellibranchiata*, or "plate-gilled," is in allusion to the gills, or organs of respiration, being in the form of leaves, or thin plates. These useful organs are perhaps better known to us in the so-called "beard" of the oyster. The body of all bivalves—that is to say, the internal organs—is wrapped up in a tough integument, technically called the "mantle." This mantle is a most useful apparatus, for it has the power of secreting the carbonate of lime held in solution by sea-water, and out of it forming the shells. Whenever the latter get damaged, also, it has the means of repairing them. The lobes of this mantle generally unite, and leave two openings, through which certain tubes or siphons pass, as in the sand-mussel. The foot of bivalves is not the important member it is with the gasteropods, where it is used as a means of locomotion. Occasionally, it is employed in digging in the soft sands, or in making short leaps, as with the common cockle. In the mussel, the foot has the power of secreting a kind of mucus, which soon hardens and forms the *byssus* (better known to us as the "moss"), by means of which the mussel is enabled to anchor its shell to the rocky sea-bottom. In all bivalves there are certain muscles called "adductor muscles," which are under the control of the animal, and used for closing the two shells together. How powerful these are, everybody knows who has tried to open an oyster—the oysterman being obliged to cut them in two with his sharp knife before he can open the shells. Of course, these muscles require to be very firmly attached to the interior of the shells, and such is the case, for we find that in dead shells, after the animal matter has been entirely removed, there are left the distinct impressions of the muscular scars. Formerly, bivalve shells were classed in two groups, according as they had two of these scars, or only one. It will be seen, therefore, that an attention to these scars, and their number and position, affords one good means of identifying species. Again, the margin of the mantle has also a muscular property, and it frequently leaves its impression in the interior of the shell as well, forming what is called the "pallial" line. An attention to this line is useful. In some bivalves we find it unbroken, when we know that in them the mantle-lobes were quite free. But, where the pallial line is indented, this is taken as an indication that the mantle-lobes were united to each other. It affords the knowledge, at the same time, that the animal had siphons, which could be withdrawn into the shell. This class of bivalves generally live in sand or mud, in which they bury themselves, leaving the siphons just protruding above. These are usually double, one being for the purpose of admitting fresh sea-water, and the other for excretory purposes. The water thus admitted not only brings food to the animal, but aerates its gills with oxygen as well. The sexes are usually distinct in bivalves, and there is occasionally a slight difference in the shells to indicate them. Thus, in the oyster, the male shell generally has the umbone, or plate near the beak, white and humpy—a fact worth knowing to oyster-eaters who don't care about "green" natives.

There is no doubt that the commonest objects along our coasts are the cockles and mussels—and a good thing for us that such is the case. The former is too well known to need description, but we have other species, some of which are much larger and handsomer than the edible one. In all, the foot of the living animal is very brilliantly coloured, generally with vermilion. The mussels have an enormous power of increase, or they could never withstand the ravages made on them. In deeper water we have a kind popularly called "Horse-mussels" (*Modiola*), whose detached shells may often be gathered after a storm. One species belonging to this is really very pretty, and is called *M. tulipa*, on account of the part about the beak being coloured with streaks of crimson or violet, like the painted petals of a tulip. Associated with the above objects, the visitor will scarcely fail to find the more brittle valves of the "Razor-shell," or "Gaper" (*Solen ensis*), as it is also called (Fig. 114). There are several species, of which that just named is the commonest. The popular name is a good guide to their identification, for the two closed valves exactly resemble a razor-handle. They do not close at either end, hence their other name of "Gaper." All the species burrow in the sand, and generally live in the same burrow during the whole of their existence, ascending and descending in it as occasion may require, and indicating their situation by the jets of sand and water they are in the habit of throwing out. The animals are said to form one of the most toothsome of our mollusca.

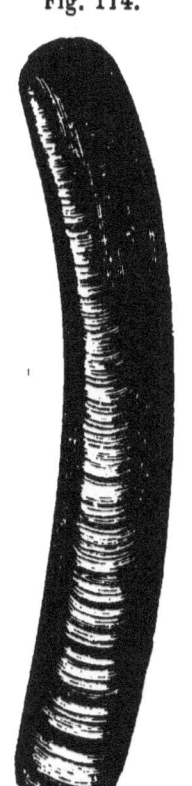

Fig. 114.

*Solen ensis.*

The "Scallop-shells" (*Pecten*) are perhaps the greatest favourites among our native bivalves. We may see them turned to all kinds of ornamental uses in the pin-cushions, &c., sold in the sea-side bazaars. There are several species, some of which are very abundant. Among these perhaps *Pecten varius* (Fig. 115) and *Pecten opercularis* are the best known. The former takes its name from its extreme variability as regards colour. It is, however, generally some shade of red or dark brown. It may be known by having only one process, called the "ear," and also by its numerous ribs, each of which has small spiny projections. It is the latter species (*P. opercularis*) which commonly goes by the name of the "Scallop." This was the shell formerly used by pilgrims, who stuck one in their hats as a sign they had been to the Holy Land. It is easily known by its *two* ears, and also by its fewer, but broader ribs, eighteen to twenty in number. The "Scallops" attain their largest size on our southern coasts, where they are esteemed great dainties when properly cooked. Their mode of progression is very peculiar, and is achieved by repeated snappings or shuttings of the two valves together; the water thus suddenly expelled projecting the bivalve in the opposite direction. All of them are very tenacious of life, and some strange stories are told of the way in which they cling to it. There can be little doubt this species is one of the handsomest, if not the handsomest, of our British bivalves. Mr. Gosse, in speaking of it, says: "It is a very pretty sight to see a healthy Pecten in a vessel of clear sea-water. The elegant valves are opened to a considerable width, perhaps to half an inch or more, and the entire aperture all round is filled by a curtain, which drops from one to the other, perpendicularly, a little way within the

Fig. 115.

*Pecten varius.*

margin. This is the mantle, and it is generally painted with rich colours, in irregular patterns, often of spots and marbled clouds of black on a rich green ground, or pearly green clouds on flesh colour —sometimes pale yellow clouds on velvet black; but these hues have no perceptible relation to those of the shell. Looking closely, you see that the mantle is not single, but composed of two curtains, whose edges meet in the middle. And now these are slightly separating, and giving us a peep into the interior. But the most notable thing we see is the array of long white taper tentacles which proceed from each edge, and wave to and fro in the clear water; while another row of similar organs, but larger, is affixed to each curtain along the line where it starts from the shell. And along this same line, scattered between the bases of the larger tentacles, there is a row (and a corresponding one on the other curtain) of beads, which seem to be turned out of the richest and most lustrous gems. Even the unassisted eye is arrested by their flashing brilliance, but with a powerful lens they look like rubies set in sockets of sapphire, from which the light blazes forth in incomparable brilliance! These are the Pecten's eyes, each of which possesses all the parts requisite for perfect vision."

It may be that the observant sea-side visitor, in the course of rambles, stumbles across a piece of old wreck that has been cast ashore. The thought is suggested as to the fate of the goodly ship to which it formerly belonged, and it is not difficult to imagine the fearful storm that broke her to pieces, and perhaps consigned her gallant crew to a watery grave! That piece of wood has probably been cast to and fro for weeks, before it reached this settlement. In the meantime, marine animals, sea-worms, zoophytes, &c., have anchored themselves to it. But what is most striking, perhaps, is the manner with which it is perforated, evidently by worm tubes. For a long time, the creatures which bored these tunnels were believed to be worms, and to this day they go by the popular name of "Shipworms" (*Teredo navalis*). They are molluscs, however, and bivalves, although the two shells, being small and by no means able to cover the soft body of the animal, were formerly regarded as the *jaws* of the worm! Each of the tubes is lined with a thin layer of shelly matter.

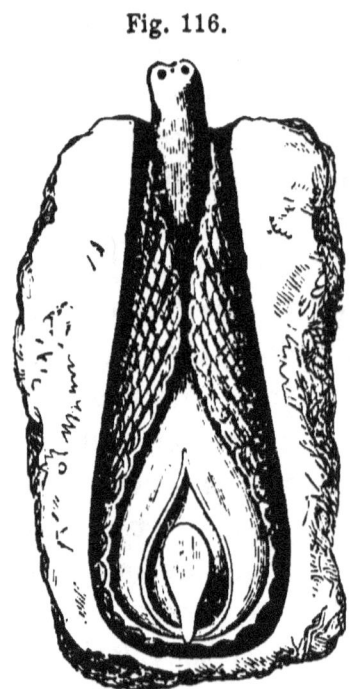

Fig. 116.

*Pholas dactylus.*

Boring mollusca are tolerably plentiful in our seas. Perhaps the principal kind is the *Pholas* (Fig. 116), whose brittle, roughened, white shells you may frequently see thrown on the sands. Or, if you are more curious, at low water you may see the animal itself ensconced in the habitation it has made. No other mollusc has had so much written about it as this. Theories innumerable have been propounded to account for the way in which it excavated hollows in the hardest and the softest rocks alike. It has been suggested that it secreted an acid, but no acid was ever found in the animal; and again, it must be a peculiar one that would dissolve away all kinds of rock. Then it was contended that the foot was covered with flinty spicules, with which the *Pholas* managed to rasp away the rock. Unfortunately, the microscope showed no traces of these flinty teeth! Here again the aquarium has contributed materially to natural history, for by its means the *Pholas* has been carefully watched, and the manner with which it mines its holes is no longer a secret. To understand how this is effected, it will be necessary first to attend to a few points in the anatomy of the animal. The external shell is white, and open at each end. Out of one end proceeds a long tube or siphon, which communicates with the aperture of the boring, and, being contractile, can squirt out a jet of water, when irritated, to some distance. At the other end of the valves is the fleshy foot, which can attach itself to the bottom of the tunnel, or to the rock. The valves at this end are much thicker than at the other, and are further strengthened by a chambered structure they possess. The exterior, also, is very rough and rasp-like. The shell is composed of that form of carbonate of lime termed *arragonite*, which is much harder and more endurable than the ordinary kind. The foot being attached, the animal keeps up a constant swaying to and fro, in a semicircular fashion, bringing the rasp-like ends of the valves to act mechanically on the rock. Meantime the siphon is busy squirting forth the water containing the fine mud thus abraded away. This is the simple means by which the *Pholas* manages to make its tunnel, as witnessed several times in the aquarium. Mr. Robertson, who exhibited Pholades in the act of boring into the chalk, has described the means as "A living combination of three instruments, viz., hydraulic apparatus, a rasp, and a syringe!" There is yet another kind of borer, much smaller in size, which literally honeycombs the seaward faces of limestone rocks, and causes no small denudation of them, by burrowing. This is the *Saxicava*, of which there are several species. The shell is very brittle, and covered with sharp wrinkles or ridges. The common name given to the *Pholas* by fishermen is "Piddock." Several species are found in the rocks of the British coast.

Strewn almost everywhere on the sands, in the spaces between high and low water, are certain shells, generally devoid of strong markings, smooth, and having only delicate shades of pink colouring to recommend them. These are the *Mactras*, or

HALF AN HOUR WITH SHELL-FISH (BIVALVES). 217

"Trough-shells," and the *Tellinas*—the commonest bivalves, next to the cockles and mussels, of our English seas. The former of these two genera is generally the larger, and may easily be identified by the structure of the hinge, which is more elaborate than that of the Tellina, having a tolerably deep nick on each side the tooth of the beak. By attending to the structure of the hinges, the student may easily learn the difference in the genera of shells, as

Fig. 117.

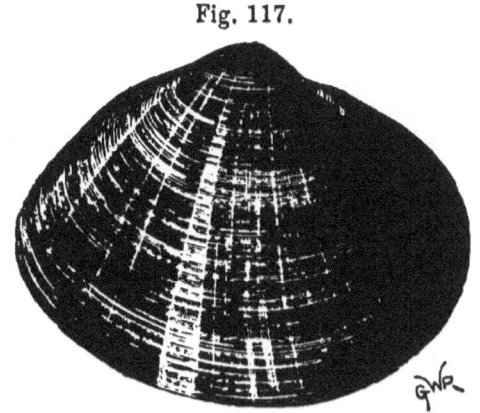

*Mactra stultorum.*

this and the scar-impressions of the muscles inside are related to anatomical differences. One species, *Mactra stultorum* (Fig. 117), is tolerably large, and abundant off all our sandy shores, especially in the north of England. In colour it is exceedingly variable, but one feature is generally constant—the presence of white bands radiating from the beak to the margin of the shell, as seen in the illustration. Another species, *Mactra truncata*, is also common;

but this shell, as its specific name indicates, is shortened or truncated on one side. Its valves, also, are more convex, and are covered with delicate grooves. Of the Tellens (*Tellinas*) there are many species common to our seas, all of which are very pretty, abounding in the sandy muds. The largest of them is the "Thick Tellen" (*Tellina crassa*, Fig. 118), which is two inches in length, of a whitish colour, with pink or red rays. The "Thin Tellen" (*Tellina tenuis*) is about the commonest of sea-side objects, and one easily recognisable by its flattened appearance, its polished surface, its thin shells, beautifully tinted inside and out with light rose colour, and, externally, also, with bands of red. The *Tellina incarnata* is much larger than the above, and narrower in proportion to its greater size. It is confined generally to the southern coasts, where its shape and colour soon introduce it to notice. The latter is frequently orange, with streaks of pink and white diversifying it. In the German Ocean, and off the eastern coasts more particularly, is another Tellen—*Tellina solidula*, or *Balthica*. It is remarkable for being a very abundant fossil shell in our boulder clay deposits (Fig. 119). It literally swarms in the Baltic Sea (whence its name), and seems to delight in any sea-water that is rendered a trifle brackish

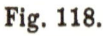
Fig. 118.

*Tellina crassa.*

by melted snow or ice, as that of the north frequently is. It is not so brilliantly coloured as the species we have just mentioned, but has the same generally diffused pink hue.

*Donax* is a bivalve nearly allied to the former. One species (*anatinus*) is very abundant with us. The animal which forms the shell has a stout yellow foot, and a frilled mantle. When the empty shell is examined along its inner margin, the latter is seen to be milled, like the edge of a new shilling. When alive, or when the empty shells have been cast ashore shortly after death, the colour is a pale olive, which is that of the investing mem-

Fig. 119.

*Tellina Balthica.*

Fig. 120.

*Donax politus.*

brane. In old and dead shells, when this is removed, the colour is white, with light purple shadings. *Donax politus* (Fig. 120) may be distinguished from the foregoing by the white bands which radiate from the beak.

220 HALF AN HOUR WITH SHELL-FISH (BIVALVES).

In the *Psammobias* this style of ornamentation is so characteristic and beautiful, that Mr. Wood has called them "Sunset-shells," in allusion to the broadening rays of coloured light which are seen during a fine sunset. In them the rays are pink on

Fig. 121.

*Mya arenaria.*

Fig. 122.

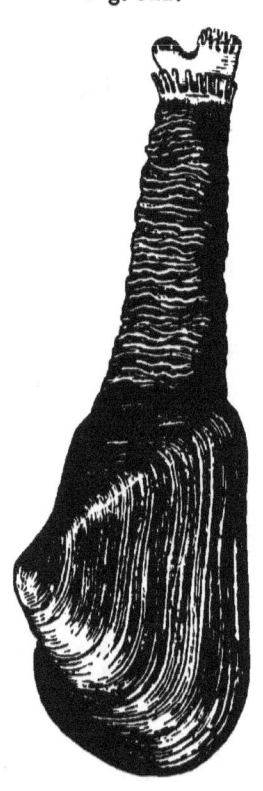

*Mya truncata.*

a yellow or red ground. They are obtained alive only by dredging, although one species is often found ashore, called *tellinella*.

The "Sand-mussel" (*Mya arenaria*) has already

been alluded to (Fig. 121). This shell may frequently be found at low water, buried near the lowest ebb, in the sands in an upright position, with its skinny siphon or tube protruding. Empty shells are also to be picked up on the beach, and may be recognised by the large hinge, one shell having an enormous toothed projection, and the other a corresponding depression. They are frequently called "Gaper-shells," because, when denuded of the external skin, the shells will not meet at one end. In the "Truncated" species (*Mya truncata*), one side of the shell is much abbreviated or truncated, and the siphon much longer (Fig. 122). This species has a northern distribution, reaching its southern limits on our coasts. *Thracia* is a genus of bivalves having some relation to the foregoing, and possessing a large hinge, with a peculiar structure. One shell is humpy, and the other nearly flat; both are very fragile. The "Otter-shells" (*Lutraria*) are the largest of British bivalves, some of them averaging as much as five inches in length. They resemble the "Razor-shells" in some respects, principally in their inability to close the ends of their shells. They are, however, more nearly allied to *Mactra*. All the "Otter-shells" live in the mud, almost completely imbedded there. There are several species living in our seas, the commonest of which is *elliptica*.

*Tapes* is a genus of bivalves, beautifully coloured, and which is further adorned with fine lines that sculpture the surface (Fig. 123). One species, abundant in our seas, *decussata*, has these lines deeper than the rest, cut into the shell much after the way in which a flat file is cut in opposite crossing lines. In the species *pullastra* (Fig. 124) the sculpturing is much more delicate and finer, and the shells smaller. A handsome and not uncommon shell is the *Venus*, one species of which (*Venus fasciata*) is nearly triangular in outline, with a gently rounded base. All the way up to the beak there run a series of strong concentric ribs, so that it is a species not difficult to determine. Its colour is generally brownish, diversified agreeably with purplish bands running down and crossing the ribs aforesaid. The foot is white, and the animal possesses two tubes or siphons for breathing water in and out. There are several species living in our seas, all of which are pretty objects. In one (*Venus verrucosa*) the surface of the valves is covered with deep furrows. *Cytherea chione* is a handsome mollusc allied to the latter, which lives in deep water, especially off the southern coasts. Its colour is chestnut-brown, having bands of paler hue radiating from the beak. *Artemis exoleta* is another related bivalve, whose large, thick, solid shells are beautifully ornamented with bands of pink and light

Fig. 123.

*Tapes aurea.*

Fig. 124.

*Tapes pullastra.*

yellow rays. In shape it is nearly round, having the beak on one side. There are several British species of this genus. Very characteristic of the northern seas are the *Astartes*, of which we have several. One of them, called *sulcata*, is exceedingly variable in colour and form. The surface of the valve is alternately ridged and furrowed; hence the specific name. In *compressa*, another species, the name again is a good indication of the chief feature about it, as the shells are flat or compressed. The latter are only about half an inch in length. The hinge of all the *Astartes* is very strong and peculiarly formed, occupying more space than is usual in shells of so small a size. Living under pretty nearly the same circumstances, only resembling the Artemis in shape and general appearance, is the *Lucina*, of which one species, *borealis*, reaches its northern limit in our seas. It is an elegant little shell, ornamented with fine concentric lines. Allied to a few of the foregoing, as regards its northern character, but much larger in size, is the *Cyprina Islandica* Indeed, this is one of our largest and stoutest shells, well proportioned, and having very stout and strong hinge-teeth. Not unfrequently it attains a length of four to five inches. It is most abundant on our northern coasts, and off those of North Wales. When recently thrown ashore, it is covered with a dark olive-brown membrane. This is another of the species peculiar to some of our boulder clays, or "glacial" deposits.

*Crenella*, on the other hand, is a bivalve only half an inch in length, of a pale green colour. There are several British species, of which one, called *discors*, is covered with delicate lines, radiating from the beak, or umbone, to the margin. The interior edges of this margin are "milled" like a shilling—or rather, *crenulated*, as the technical word has it. It is this feature which gives the name to the genus, although, as we have already seen, it is shared by other bivalves. *Crenella* may be found entangled in the roots of the large seaweeds (*Laminaria*) which are cast ashore. It forms a curious nest or cocoon, spun out of its byssus, and having stones, &c., adhering to it and hiding it. The *Lima* resembles it in this queer habit, although it differs much from it in appearance. It has a surface cut like a file, and is a very fragile and elegant shell. The valves gape, and do not come quite together when shut.

Two other British bivalves, *Nucula* and *Leda*, may be known by the structure of their hinge-teeth, which are very numerous and pretty. In the former, there is a nacreous or pearly lining to the interior of the shell, which is only about half an inch in length. *Leda* is longer and more elegantly shaped. A series of shells not likely to be mistaken are the "Arks" (*Arca*), so called on account of their chest-like form. One species, *tetragona*, is deep and squarish. The exterior is furrowed and ridged. There are several British species, which may be found at low water under stones, or hiding up in the empty shells of other molluscs. Perhaps one of the most striking of all our native bivalves is one that is common on our southern coasts, although less plentiful elsewhere, called *Pectunculus glycimeris* (Fig. 125). It is two inches across, nearly round in shape, having numerous strong hinge-teeth, which radiate from each side the centre. The exterior is covered with fine lines running down to the margin, and over all there is a series of zig-zag, red markings, which produce a very pretty effect. It is on the southern coasts also, and we believe there alone, that we obtain the *Pinna*, the largest of British bivalves, as it sometimes attains the length of twelve inches, anchoring itself by means of a long silken byssus. Mr. Couch says that these beautiful shells, off the Cornish coast, "stud the bottom in multitudes, with only two or three inches of the pointed end inserted in the mud." One end of the shells—the broad end—cannot be closed by *art;* but Mr. Couch, quoting Montagu, the celebrated conchologist, says of it: "The animal is capable of effecting it, and observation has taught me that this is its method of obtaining food. In its ordinary position this opening is about two inches wide, exposing the contained animal, which occupies but a small portion of the cavity, and seems to offer

Fig. 125.

*Pectunculus glycimeris.*

Q

itself as a prey to the first creature that may choose to devour it. Some fish are thus tempted to enter, but the first touch within is the signal for its destruction. The shell closes not only at the side but top, the latter action being effected by the separation of the pointed ends; and the captive is either crushed to death, or soon perishes from confinement."

Of the oyster we do not presume to speak. Internally and externally, it is too well known to need description. But we often see attached to it—and not to it only, but to other large shells, stones, &c. —what seems to be a miniature oyster. This is the *Anomia*, whose thin, glassy valves mould themselves to the objects they cling to. On examining the lower valve, near the beak will be seen a hole, through which, in the living state, a fleshy plug passes, by means of which the animal is enabled to attach itself. The inexorable limits of space forbid us attempting more than drawing attention to the commonest shells, and those most likely to be found at all rocky bathing-places. Underneath the stones, at low water, may be found several minute species, as *Kellia, Lepton, Montacuta*, &c. The former loves to hide itself among the roots of seaweed, or in any sheltered situation; the second is a thin, flat, bivalve; and the third usually adheres to the roots of the larger seaweeds. Off our southern coasts, also, may be found the pretty little *Galeomma*, whose pearly white hue is sure to recommend it as an object of beauty. In conclusion, it will be seen that we have species enough in our British seas, and those not difficult to get at, to form a really attractive cabinet. Few objects are more admired, and none look better when well arranged and properly named, than marine shells, whether univalves or bivalves. They have an association, also, which is not to be despised; for they remind us of sunny days by the salt sea, when the invigorating air filled our lungs, and took years off our age in a few hours! They bring to our recollection happy hours, dead friends, days never to return; and thus inanimate objects may minister to our higher feelings, and make the past live again in more than its original enjoyment.

## XIII.

### HALF AN HOUR WITH CRUSTACEA.

WE have already remarked on the wonderful transformations which a patient study of marine animals has brought to light. The metamorphosis by which an ugly grub is transformed, as if by magic, into a gorgeous butterfly is more than equalled among the jelly-fish. Not less marvellous are the changes which take place in the life-history of the Crustacea. The study of the latter has been much pursued in this country and France during the last quarter of a century. As usual, creatures which were formerly considered distinct species, or genera, are now classed as merely different stages in the development of the same animal. More, the *plan* on which such well-known objects as crabs and lobsters are constructed is found to run more or less through the whole of the Crustacea. This similarity of construction, however, is not plainly visible until all the stages in the development of the animal, from the egg to the adult, have been noted.

Who, for instance, would ever dream of finding a second cousin to the lobster in the barnacles, which encrust our rocks so as to render walking over them almost impossible? Or find, in the stalked barnacles, which we see attached to the piece of drifted wreck, a similar relationship? In some respects, to the eye these animals seem real molluscs, or shell-fish, the latter kind especially. You examine one and find that the stalk is a muscular tube, to the summit of which two or more large shells, not unlike the valves of Tellina, enclose long, feathery tentacles. The shells are tinted light blue, and, when detached, have much of the look of ordinary bivalves. Or, bestow a moment's extra attention on the common acorn-shells (*Balanus*) which encrust the stones, rocks, and larger bivalve mollusca. They well deserve their popular name, for, in outward shape, the entire structure is not unlike the upper half of an acorn. These, you see, have no stalk, but are attached to their places by the base of the shell, so as to be called "sessile." Like the true barnacle, each individual domicile is composed of several parts, hence the name of "multivalve" was given to them when they were regarded as mollusca. There is one barnacle (*Scalpellum vulgare*) which has the valve nearly oval. When these open, a hand of bristly tentacles is hastily thrust forth, and as suddenly drawn in again. This species is small, and not unfrequently is found attached to the bases of a cluster of Corallines. The larger species, and that which we have mentioned as clustering on old wrecks, &c., is the *Lepas anatifera*, about which the tale was formerly told, and firmly believed in, that they were descended from a species of goose, and that, in turn, they brought forth geese! We have seen old prints in which the artist has endeavoured to illustrate this idea. Attention has been drawn to the law of "alternation of generations" in many marine animals, so that we are prepared beforehand not to be greatly surprised at anything marvellous; but this ancient belief transcends all we have yet told! The stalk of this species is from eight inches to a foot in length, and is tough and leathery, having muscles running through it which contort it and cause the whole organism to wave to and fro in the water like a tall tree in a high wind. This species it is which, in warmer seas, so greatly infests ships' bottoms as to render navigation difficult. When that part of the animal enclosed within the valves is watched, there will be seen to emerge a hand-like member, the fingers of which are beautifully feathered. It is this striking resemblance to a feather which perhaps first suggested the fable about its being a transformed goose. The colour of the feathery fingers is purplish-black, and about three-quarters of an inch in length. When put out, they snap at and curl round any organism that may serve them as food, and immediately jerk it to the mouth, closing their valves after them. The "Acorn-shells," or sessile barnacles (*Balanus balanoides*), are abundant everywhere—perhaps a trifle too much so, you will be inclined to think, when you find that their sharp edges have clean cut through your wetted boots as you were zoologising among the rock-pools at low water! You notice that each piece of the shell is chambered at the base, and the whole of them form a conical structure, the top of which is closed by two other pieces of shell which meet in the middle, and open and shut like the folding doors of a street cellar. These are thrown open, exactly as cellar doors are by a person beneath, and out pops a feathery hand that snaps at prey and secures it, as in the stalked barnacles.

And now we beg the reader's attention to the metamorphoses of these curious animals, when it will be seen that, little as they resemble crustacea when full-grown, they show certain affinities to them when juvenile. The first stage in their life-history is that the young assumes the form and appearance of an Entomostracan, or "Water-flea," having a *single* eye, two pairs of antennæ, and a forked tail. It subsequently moults several times, assuming a different appearance each time. At the third time it resembles a *Cypris*, and is enclosed within two valves, and has two eyes instead of one. Its great search now seems to be for rocks, timber, &c., and having met with any of these, it exudes a sort of glue and attaches itself. Another moult takes place, the valves are thrown off, and the adult form is assumed. The creature is, in fact, attached by its antennæ, and has what in other crustacea would be legs—the same organs modified into the feathery hand of which we have spoken. The fingers of this hand are called " cirri," and, as they represent actual feet, the Barnacle family go by the name of *Cirripedia*.

The true crustacea, such as our lobsters, crabs, prawns, shrimps, &c., differ very much among themselves, whilst their young, or larva, are still more unlike their parents, and bear a resemblance to the young of *Cirripedia*. It is just possible that our readers may be better acquainted with the taste and flavour of the former animals than with their general structure or anatomy, therefore a few words of explanation may not be deemed out of place, before we refer to some of the commoner members of this group which the sea-side student may come across in his rambles. None of the crustacea have real jaws, but instead, the feet are modified to carry on the process of mastication. The typical crustacean is supposed to have its limy shell formed out of twenty-one pieces. These are distributed in three divisions, called respectively the head, the thorax, and the abdomen, seven in each. In many cases, as in the crabs, &c., the fourteen segments of the head and chest are fused, or run together into one great piece, called the "cephalo-thorâx." These types of crustacea sometimes go by the name of "Stalk-eyed," on account of the eyes being borne on pedicels, or stalks, capable of moving about. Another general name for them is *Decapoda*, or "ten-footed," in allusion to the number of limbs. The entire series is capable of being subdivided into two great groups, called the *macrura* and the *brachyura*—the "long-tailed" crustaceans, as the lobsters, and "short-tailed," as the crabs. In the latter, the great broad shield covering the head, &c., is termed the *carapace*, the so-called tail being in reality the abdomen. In the crabs, this is reduced to a mere rudiment, and is always tucked under the carapace, the vulgar name for it being the "apron." Although the twenty-one segments of the body of a crustacean are modified in such a singular manner, they are never wholly lost sight of. Even when they are fused together, they can be told by the pairs of appendages. We have already spoken of the mouth as having no real jaws, but modified feet. The hinder pair of the mouth appendages are so little altered in appearance as to be called "foot-jaws." The first three pairs of legs placed under the carapace are usually armed with nippers—the organs placed under the abdomen, or tail, being termed "swimmerets," because these are used, like the boards of a paddle-wheel, in moving about in the water. The mouth of a crab or lobster opens into a globular stomach, which is furnished with a calcareous apparatus for triturating food. The heart is placed along the back, and is therefore called *dorsal;* the nervous system being arranged beneath, or in the *ventral* part of the body. Perhaps the most wonderful arrangement in the structural economy of the crustacea is in their mode of breathing. If you examine a tolerably large lobster, you will find that beneath the broad carapace the plates forming it do not quite meet, and that the edges are not fastened. The legs are articulated to the under side, and as the *gills*, or branchiæ, are placed within this large plate, beneath, and air can only be supplied by fresh sea-water, it follows that every time the legs are moving about, in swimming or otherwise, they are pumping fresh air to the gills, as well as serving for locomotive purposes.

Commencing with the crabs, it is to be observed that these animals are not met with in high latitudes. They are most abundant in seas that are warmer than our own, abounding in tropical regions, and attaining their northern boundary in our own seas, where they are far from uncommon, either in species or individuals. Among these, the group called "Spider-crabs," on account of their long, spider-like legs, are perhaps the most abundant, and may be found lurking under stones, &c., at low water. One of these, commonly called the "Corwich" (*Maia squinado*), Fig. 126, lives in deeper water, and is a great trouble to the fishermen, as it enters the crab and lobster pots and eats up the bait, and by its restless moving about frightens away the crustacea which the fisherman is endeavouring to entrap. In this species the carapace is ovoid and set all over with spines, whence its name. A great difference in appearance, however, results from the difference in age of the individuals. It is a very common species, and sometimes is as much as eight inches in length. In many places it is eaten by the poorer classes as food, but it is said to be vapid and coarse in flavour. These crabs make their appearance very suddenly, and often in great swarms, about the month of May.

Fig. 126.

Spiny Spider-crab (*Maia squinado*).

Another common species, and one of the largest of British crabs, is *Hyas araneus* (Fig. 127), a crustacean well known from the seaweeds and zoophytes which grow on and nearly cover its carapace. The seaweeds are generally red ones, and so the crab is well concealed by them. It was formerly thought that the animal dressed itself up in this fantastic garb, but it is now known that they grow naturally upon it. All the slow-moving crabs are liable to similar parasitic growths, and the so-called "Spider-

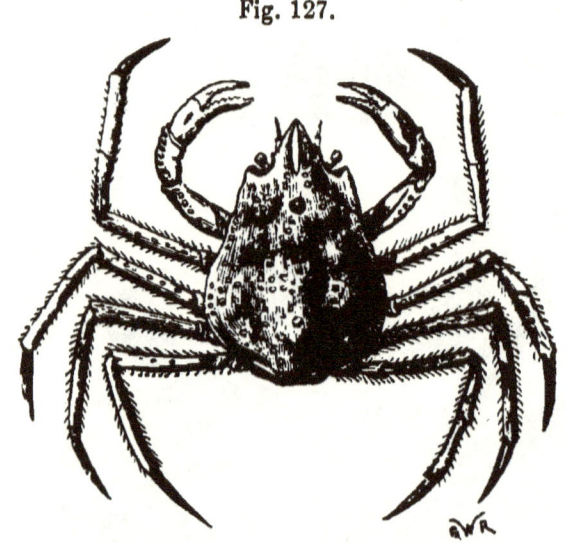

Fig. 127.

The Spider-crab (*Ilyas araneus*).

crabs" especially. One of the latter, known as the "Long-legged Spider-crab" (*Stenorynchus phalangium*), has a small, triangular carapace, not unlike a pair of kitchen bellows. Its legs are long, hairy, and quite spider-like. This is one of the most abundant of our triangular crabs, and is known from its frequenting the mouths of rivers. It seems to prefer tolerably deep water, but it is to be found also among the rocks at low tide. It is very sluggish in its habits, and soon dies when taken out of the water. The rays and codfish feed largely on it, and it may often be taken from the stomachs of those fish. The "Four-horned Spider-crab" (*Pisa tetraodon*, Fig. 128) has also a triangular-shaped back or carapace, with a series of strong spines

Fig. 128.

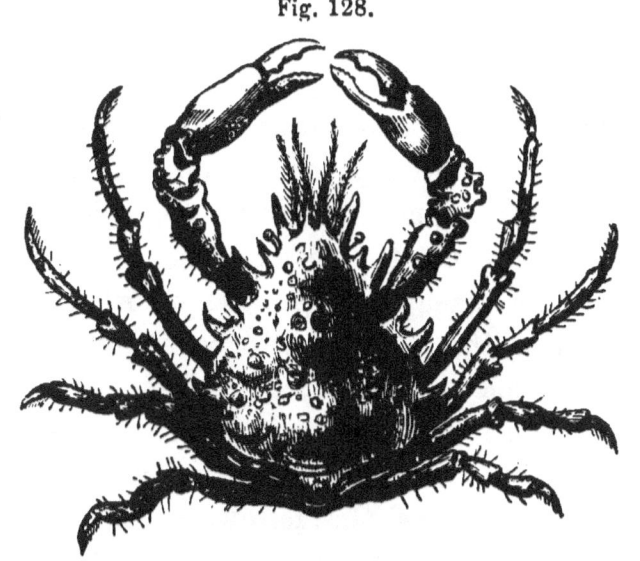

The Four-horned Spider-crab (male) (*Pisa tetraodon*), nat. size.

along the margin. The legs are shorter and stouter than in the previous species. Its name is derived from the four stout spines which project in front, near the eyes. Like the *Hyas*, it has generally a parasitic growth of algæ and zoophytes on its shield.

Of the great crab (*Cancer pagurus*) no description is needed beyond our stating that this is the common edible crab of our fishmarkets. It was evidently known to the ancient Romans by the name of *Carabus*—hence the common name, given to the whole of the short-tailed crustaceans, of "Crabs." It abounds off rocky coasts, and smaller individuals are also seen burrowing in the sands, where they will endeavour to evade notice by flattening themselves, and trying to pass for pebbles—another instance of the great law of mimicry which we find adopted so generally in the animal kingdom. The crabs live on all kinds of animal garbage, and so far are the scavengers of the deep. As is generally known, both crabs and lobsters go through a series of moultings, or casting off of the shell, before the final and full-grown stage is arrived at. The shell has not the power of being enlarged, like that of the sea-urchins, and so no other resource is left but to throw it off altogether, in order that a new one may form which shall better fit the increasing bulk of the animal parts. At certain times of the year, this moulting takes place. The Rev. J. G. Wood gives the following as shed by the lobster, in addition to the external coat:

> "The footstalks of the eyes,
> The external cornea of the eyes,
> The internal thoracic bones,
> The membrane of the ear,
> The membranous covering of the lungs,
> The tendons of the claws,
> The lining of the stomach, and
> The stomachic teeth."

Singularly enough, the male seeks the female when she is moulting; and when a female crab retires to some quiet and safe corner for the purpose of throwing off her shell, she is always attended by a male! When crabs moult they differ somewhat from their relations the lobsters in their way of effecting it. The latter draw out the body, just above the abdominal ring; but in the crabs the shell parts asunder by a suture which opens in a curved direction around the under side of the shell.

Another abundant species along our British shores is the common "Shore-crab" (*Carcinus mænas*). The wonderful manner with which this creature can walk and burrow, and partly swim, distinguishes it from its fellows. Its carapace, or shell, is covered with little tubercles, and the whole is a blackish-green colour. In the young, however, it is mottled with white. This crab may be found everywhere at low water, crouching under stones, and, when disturbed, either trying to make its way to the water, or else to suddenly bury itself in the yielding sands. It is so formed that it can live out of water longer than any other British crab, and, at the same time, it can live wholly immersed in water for days together. This crab is often sold for the last mentioned, and is much eaten in our large towns. It may always be identified by its toothed margin; that of the great, or edible crab, being frilled. As food, its flavour is good, and its flesh sweet and wholesome. It lives on the fry of fish and other crustacea, as well as upon any garbage it may come across. It has a trick of pretending to be dead when caught, and when it believes escape to be impossible. The baskets in which the edible crab are caught off the coasts of Norfolk, are usually baited with dead fresh-water fish. The "Porcelain-crab" (*Porcellana platycheles*) is a beautiful little animal, also to be found underneath the stones at low water. Its colour is reddish-brown, with pale yellow on the under side. The foreclaws are exceedingly largely developed for a crab of its size, and this is a good means of knowing it at sight. If seized by these claws it at once detaches them, and hurries off whilst you are wondering at the suicidal amputation. Another and allied species (*Porcellana longicornis*) will perhaps be met with in the same places as the former, but its small size, only a quarter of an inch in length, and especially the *inequality* in the size of its foreclaws, will prevent any mistake in its identification.

The "Pea-crabs" (Fig. 129) are worthy of notice, if not for their size, at least because they afford us an opportunity of freeing them from an ignorant suspicion which has long been attached to them. They are usually found living in the shells of bivalve mollusca, especially in those of the common mussel. Off the southern coasts they seem to favour the shells of the *Pinna* for their

Fig. 129.

The Pea-crab (*Pinnotheres pisum*).

habitation, and almost every one of the latter contains one of these little Pea-crabs inside. It is owing to their living in mussel shells the idea got abroad that it was these crabs which caused the peculiar illness called "musselling," which frequently attacks people who have eaten heartily of them. All we need say is that the notion is completely erroneous. What "musseling" is caused by is not perfectly understood, but there seems reason to believe it is due to eating them when they are in a state of decomposition. The sexes of the Pea-crab differ so remarkably that they have long been taken for different and distinct species. The "Nut-crabs" (*Ebalia*) require a sharp eye to detect them, for the largest is little over half an inch long. Their shell is lozenge-shaped, with rounded angles. All the claws are, with the exception of the foreclaws, usually tucked under the carapace, so as hardly to be visible. There are several species of this genus, not uncommon especially on our southern coasts. Like many others of the crabs, they sham death when caught, and are also so modified by "mimicry," that one is apt to take their dull white carapaces for quartz pebbles. They usually burrow in gravel, and are nocturnal in their habits. The "Angled-crab" (*Gonoplax angulatus*) well deserves its name, as it is certainly the most angular-shaped of any of our British crabs. The hind limbs are flattened, and may be used for swimming, especially as it frequents deep water. At Dublin this species goes by the name of "Coffin-crab." The

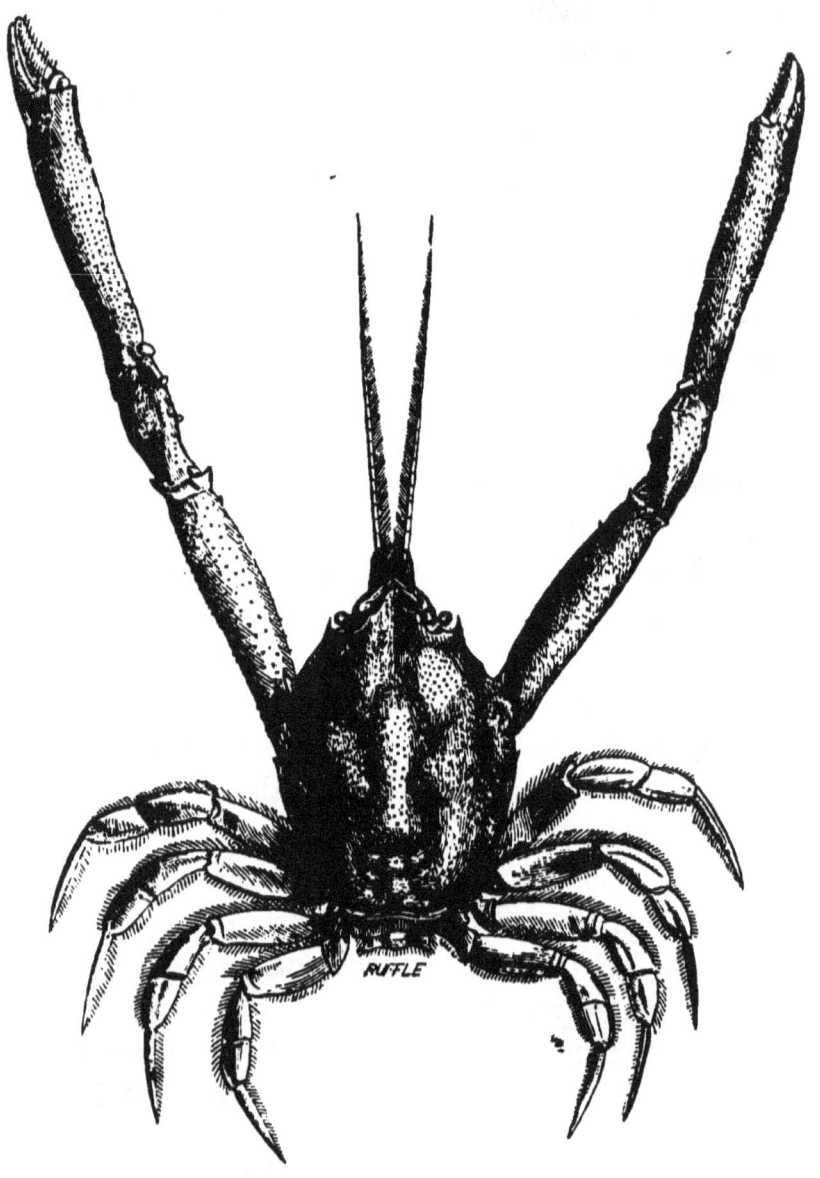

The Masked Crab (*Corystes Cassivelaunus*).  Drawn from Nature, life size.  The Male.

"Masked-crab" (*Corystes Cassivelaunus*, Figs. 130, 131) may be known from its curious habit of sitting upright, like a dog in the act of "begging." A peculiar crab, much resembling the "Spiny-crab," is a species

Fig. 131.

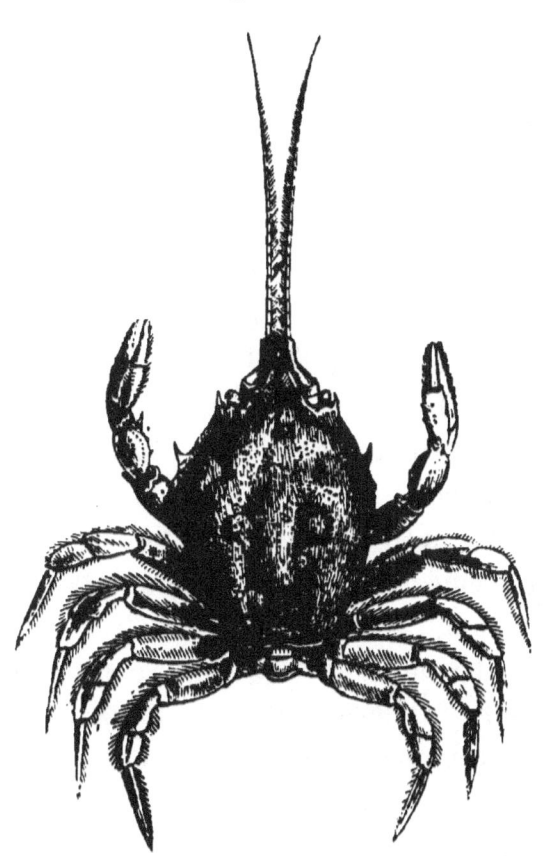

The Female.

which does not extend further south than the Isle of Man, and accordingly goes by the name of the "Northern Stone-crab" (*Lithodes maia*). It is covered all over with spines, like that species; the shell being of a pale red, and the spines of a darker hue.

There is a group of crabs which go by the name of "Swimming-crabs," and have their claws modified for the purpose of swimming, as well as crawling along the sea-bottom. One of the commonest of these is the "Velvet Swimming crab," or "Velvet Fiddler," as it is also called (*Portunus puber*). There is no difficulty in separating the crawling from the swimming crabs. The former always have the hind legs round, whilst those of the latter are flattened and oar-like. The species we have just mentioned has a broad shell, or carapace, toothed in front, with the front claws covered with little tubercles. It is bright and showily coloured, although the colours soon fade after death. Off the coasts of Devon and Cornwall this is a very common species. Its size ranges from two to three inches. Another species haunts the same habitat, but extends further along the western coasts. This is the "Cleanser Swimming-crab," whose shell is of a pale red colour. There are several other species of *Portunus* to be met with off the English coasts.

The "Hermit-crab" (*Pagurus Bernhardus*), which may be found in every heap of trawler's rubbish, is one of the most singular creatures known. It takes its name from its habit of living in the empty shells of univalve molluscs, that of the common whelk being a favourite. The great peculiarity about it is that its belly, or abdomen, is always soft, and not protected by a living crust as with the lobsters. Hence the necessity for it to make up for this important deficiency by a valuable instinct, which prompts it to seek out empty univalve shells, and to thrust into them its soft and defenceless hinder part. The fore claws are covered with the usual hard crust, one of them being longer than the other, and used to block up the hole of the shell when attacked, on the plan of an operculum. Whilst the Hermit-crab is growing, these claws, &c., moult, as in the ordinary crabs, and accordingly the animal has to pull himself out of his old lodgings, and seek another and a larger. The way in which it tries each shell by inserting its soft belly into it, just as a countryman will try on half-a-dozen pairs of boots before he is fitted, is exceedingly comical. The end of the abdomen is provided with certain appendages, by means of which it can hold on to the interior of the borrowed shell. These are under the perfect control of the animal, which can let go at will. There are nearly a dozen species of British Hermit-crabs, nearly all of which inhabit different species of empty univalves. One of these crabs (*Pagurus Prideauxi*) is remarkable for its always being accompanied by a sea-anemone; a circumstance we noticed in our chapter on sea-anemones.

In addition to the foregoing, there is a group of pigmy crustaceans common in our seas, which may be found more or less abundantly in the rock-pools at low water. These belong to the family *Pycno-*

*gonidæ*. They seem to affect the bushy tufts of the common coralline sea-weed. In appearance they are not unlike those marine crustaceans which go by the name of "Sea-spiders." They are furnished with hooked claws, instead of nippers, by means of which they are able to cling very tenaciously to any object. One of these (*Pallene pygmæa*, Fig. 132) produces larvæ which have the two foreclaws, however, provided with nippers. When placed under the microscope the movements of the stomach, &c., can be plainly seen, owing to the transparency of their bodies. Their ova is attached to the abdomen by means of false feet. They do not seem to be provided with any special organs of respiration, but the oxygenation of the blood appears to take place through the general surface of the body, which is provided with perforations set in minute tubercles that are scattered all over it, like the spiracles of an insect. Notwithstanding this, the articulation of the limbs to the body is by means of stout and strong muscles, every movement of which can be seen through the transparent integument. An allied species is *Achelia hispidata*, Fig. 133, which may be known by its smaller and more compact body, and shorter limbs, as well as by its proboscis. It also possesses a small pair of jointed antennæ. Both the foregoing little creatures live on decaying animal and vegetable matter. The true *Pycnogons*, or "Sea-spiders," are now classed as genuine crustaceans by Dr. Dohrn, who has written on their embryology. One of them (*Nymphon*

HALF AN HOUR WITH CRUSTACEA. 247

*gracile,* Fig. 134) is abundant, and said to be sometimes parasitic on jelly-fish. They may be found under the stones and roots of sea-weed at low water.

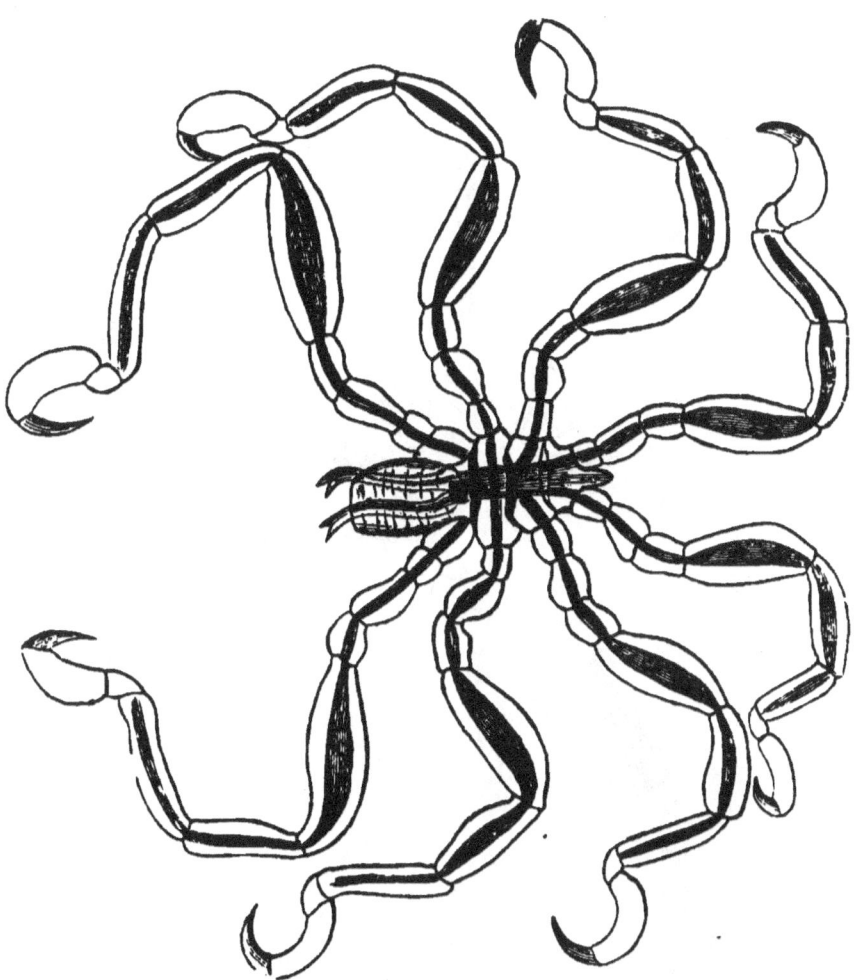

Fig. 132.—*Pallene pygmæa,* × 16.

When disturbed, they will catch hold of anything that comes in their way, and help them to escape.

Between the short-tailed and the long-tailed crustacea—crabs and lobsters—we have in our British

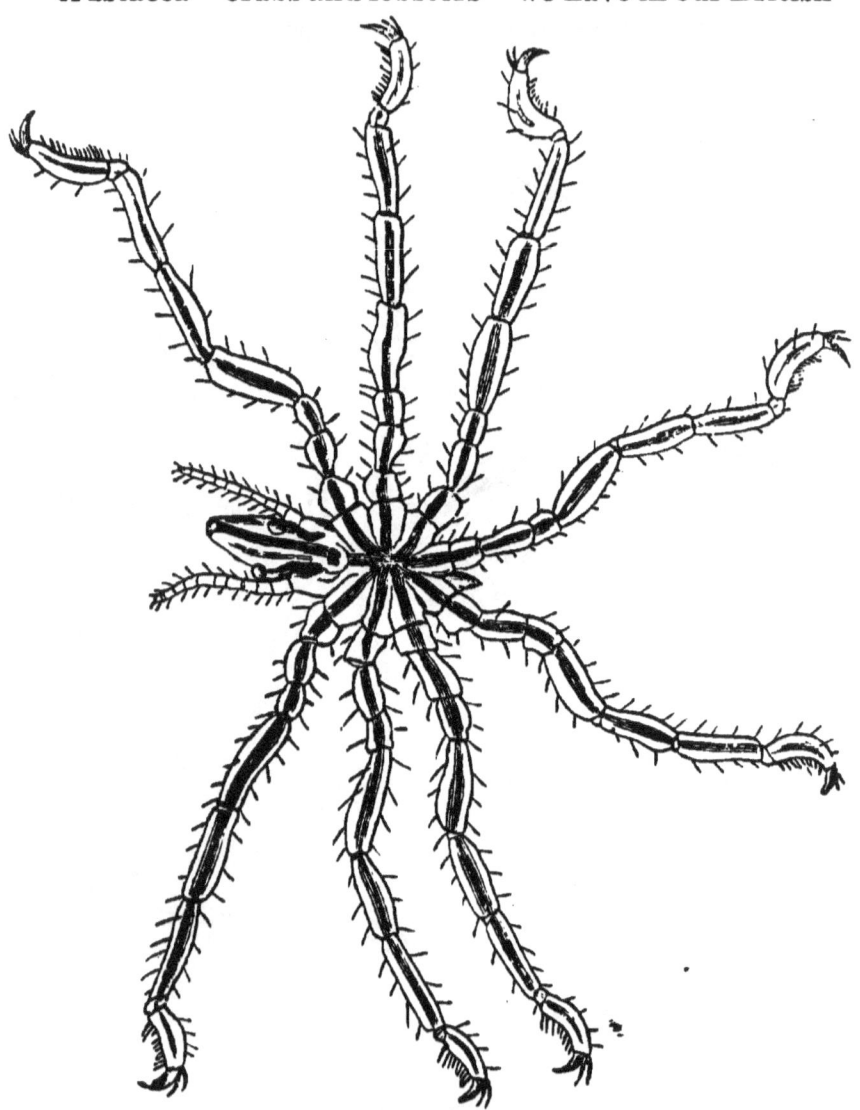

Fig. 133.—*Achelia hispidata*, × 16.

species others popularly called "Squat-lobsters" (Fig. 135), which, during rest, bend their abdomens

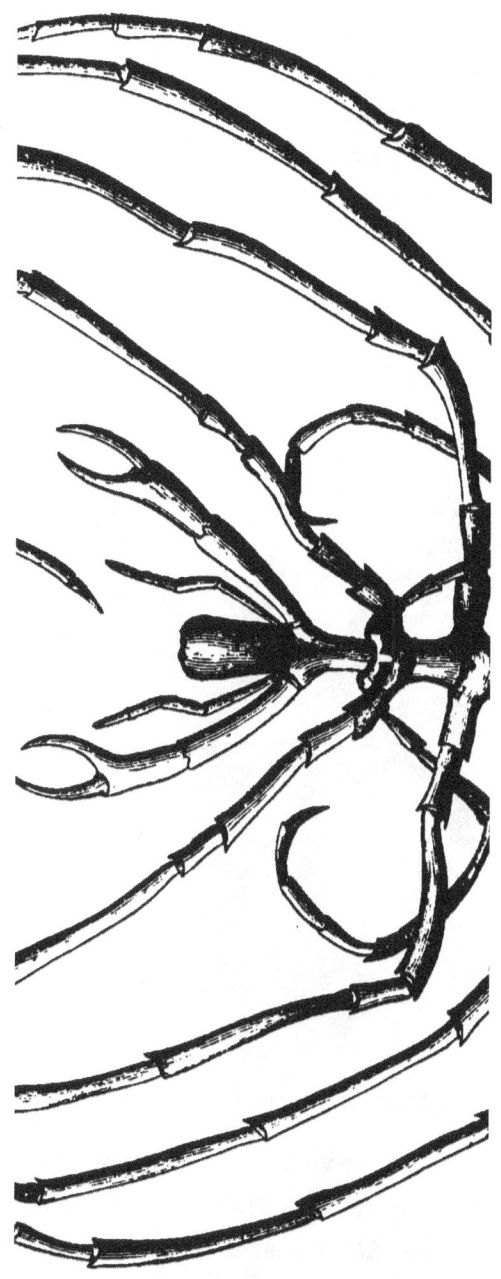

Fig. 134.—*Nymphon gracile*, × 10.

250  HALF AN HOUR WITH CRUSTACEA.

completely under the carapace, as a crab does his "apron." They are nocturnal in their habits, and love to lurk beneath stones. Some of them are gaudily coloured, and are really attractive objects; such as the "Scarlet-squat" (*Galathea nexa*), whose

Fig. 135.

The Scaly Galathea (*Galathea squamifera*).

whole length, however, is not two inches. They generally frequent deepish water, and are most abundant off the Devon and Cornish coasts.

The lobster is a good typical example of the

genuine long-tailed crustaceans, and no more needs a detailed description than the edible crab. We have already quoted from Mr. Wood as to the thorough exuviation which goes on during the moulting season. The lobster usually sheds his coat in August or September; and the chief feature about it afterwards is that it feeds most ravenously. Professor Bell has shown that it has a real parental fondness for its young, and that the latter have been seen swimming about it, as chickens follow a hen. There is ample reason to believe this statement, which was given on good evidence; for an amphipod called *Gammarus*, which abounds along our coasts, and is often caught by children in mistake for shrimps, and boiled and eaten as such, is also remarkable for her maternal solicitude for her young, the latter swimming about her as those of the lobster are said to do (see Fig. 136). The lobster swims about by means of the swimmerets, but it also uses its tail as a powerful instrument for propelling itself backwards. It is said to be able to shoot backwards as much as twenty feet by a single flap. Its eggs are usually laid in the sand, and allowed to hatch themselves. So perfectly does the lobster cast off his old coat, that the latter might be taken for a perfect animal. The " Spiny-lobster," or " Cray-fish " (*Palinurus*), is about a foot in length, and is common in the German Ocean and along western coasts. Our readers must be familiar with its spiny appearance, and light scarlet colour, as seen exposed on the fishmongers' stalls. Its flesh, however, is much inferior in flavour to that of the common lobster.

The shrimps and prawns must not be neglected in any gossip about marine crustacea. People are constantly confounding one of these with the other, perhaps on account of their nearly equal size—in fact they commonly go by the name of "red" and "brown" shrimps! There are several species of

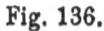

*Gammarus locusta* and her brood.

prawn abundant in our seas, and two of them (*Palæmon serratus* and *Palæmon squilla*) are often confounded with the shrimps. The difference, however, may easily be seen, in the greater number of pairs of antennæ possessed by the prawn; the shrimp having only two pair. Again, the prawns are furnished with a prolongation of the carapace between the eyes, called the *rostrum*, and in *Palæmon serratus* (Fig. 137) this is notched like a saw, whence the name. The latter attains a length of four inches,

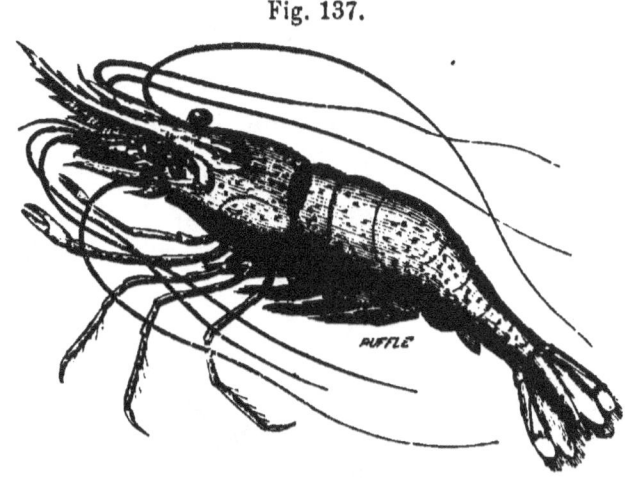

*Palæmon serratus.*

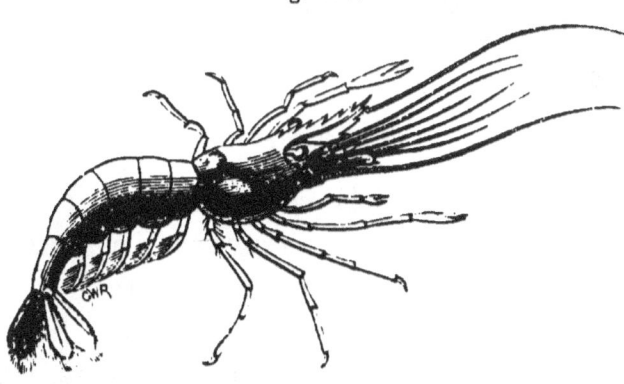

*Palæmon squilla.*

and it is when young that it gets mistaken for the shrimp. The *squilla* (Fig. 138) is smaller, and perhaps has to suffer even more through the same mistake. The common shrimp (*Crangon vulgaris*, Fig. 139) is generally distinguished, not only as the "brown shrimp," but also as the "sand-shrimp," by fishermen. It is very fond of shallow water, often swimming along the surface, and occasionally leaping out into the air. But the shrimp is most at home on the fine sandy bottom, to which the abundant minute specks of its body assimilate it in appearance. The moment it settles in the sand, it throws up sprays into the water, which gradually

Fig. 139.

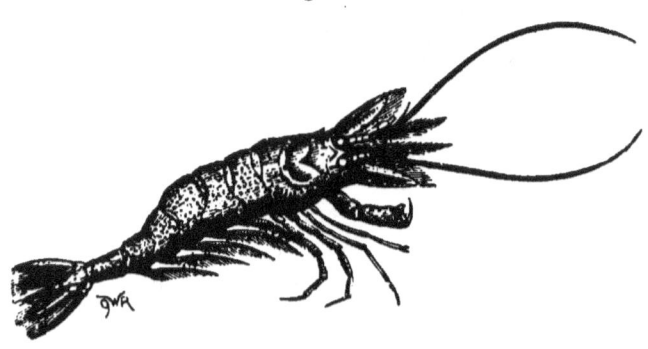

*Crangon vulgaris.*

settle down and nearly cover it up. It spawns throughout the year, the female carrying the eggs entangled among her swimming feet. The eyes are placed on the top of the head. There are several other species of shrimps in our seas, more or less common, of which the "Banded Shrimp" (*Crangon fasciatus*, Fig. 140) is one. *Pandalus annulicornis* is another prawn which, at Yarmouth, on the eastern coast, is frequently eaten as a shrimp.

It attains a length exceeding two inches, and is of reddish-grey colour, marked with deep red. The common name for it is the "Shore-prawn." Underneath the gill-covers both of shrimps and prawns may often be seen a parasitic crustacean (*Bopyrus crangorum*, Fig. 141), which often causes a peculiar bulging of the skin.

In conclusion, we would notice a group of crustaceans most abundant in the rock-pools and along the wet sands of our coasts. One of these (*Mysis chamæleon*, Figs. 142, and 143) is very abundant, and takes its name from its varying tints and colours. Its

Fig. 140.

The Banded Shrimp (*Crangon fasciatus*).

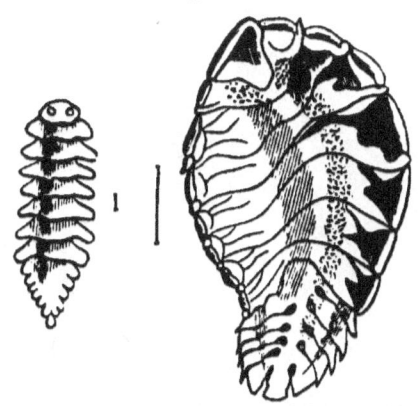

Fig. 141.

*Bopyrus crangorum*, × 10. Male and Female.

length is generally over an inch, and its stalked eyes show its relation to the shrimps. One very singular species of crustacean, *Amphithöe rubricata*, about half an inch in length, and of a brilliant crimson hue, mottled with white, may be found at the roots of Laminaria, or on the under sides of

Fig. 142.

*Mysis chamæleon,* × 3.

Fig. 143.

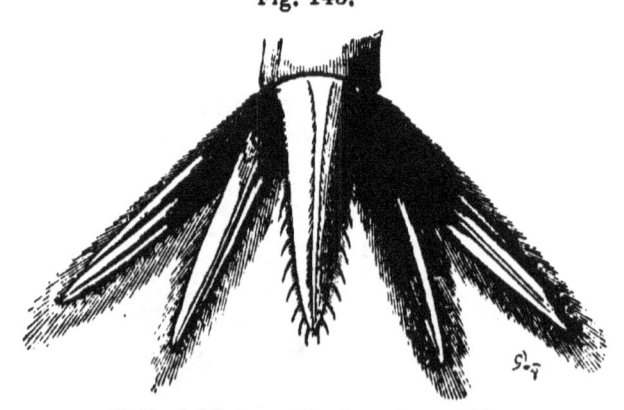

Tail of *Mysis*, with *otoconia*, ×10.

stones in a few fathoms of water. This species is remarkable for building a sort of nest with spun materials, in the smaller sea-weeds, exactly as birds do in bushes, see Fig. 144.

HALF AN HOUR WITH CRUSTACEA. 257

The "Sand-hoppers" are deservedly so called; and every sea-side visitor who has thrown himself on the yielding sands for a few minutes must have been surprised at the numbers of jumping creatures which he disturbed. The commonest of these is

Fig. 144.

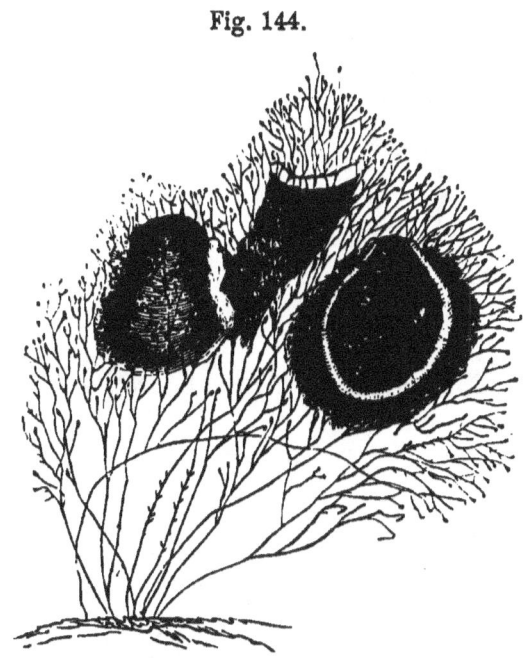

Group of nests of *Podocerus capillatus*, after Bate and Westwood.

called *Talitrus locusta* (Fig. 145), and its locust-like form will readily help to identify it. The "Shore-hoppers" are nearly allied to the above, but they may be told by their huge and highly-developed foreclaw, one only, as well as by their larger size (Fig. 146). It is very seldom these creatures enter the water; they seem much to prefer sporting on the

258    HALF AN HOUR WITH CRUSTACEA.

damp sands between the tides. Nearly allied to the shrimps are two species, termed respectively the "Night-walker" (*Nika edulis*, Fig. 147) and *Hip-*

Fig. 145.

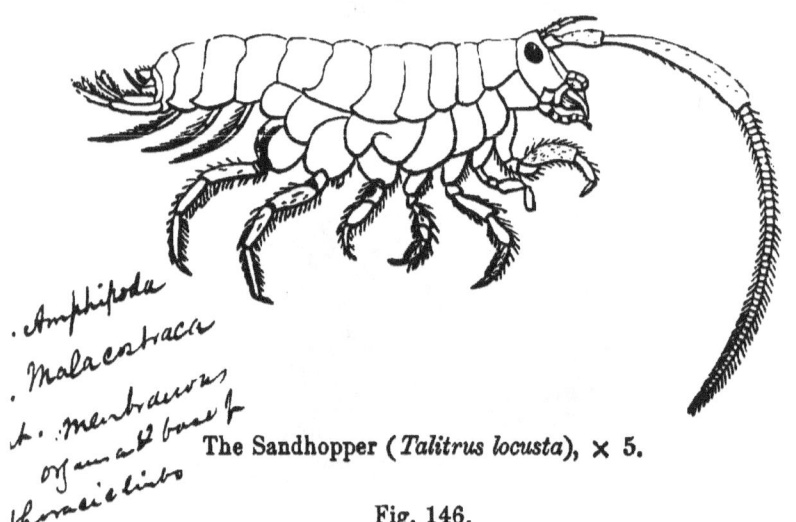

The Sandhopper (*Talitrus locusta*), × 5.

Fig. 146.

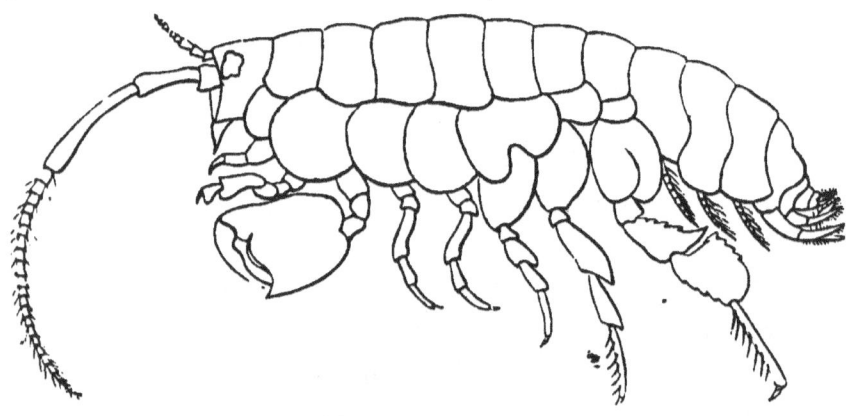

The Shorehopper (*Orchestia littorea*), × 5.

*polyte varians*, Fig. 148). The former takes its name on account of its abounding in the evening.

HALF AN HOUR WITH CRUSTACEA. 259

The latter often assumes two colours, a bright green and as bright a red. Neither is uncommon.

Fig. 147.

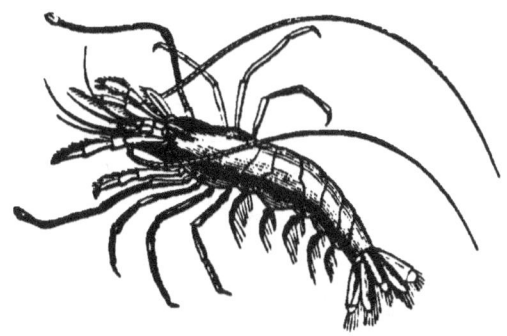

The Night-walker (*Nika edulis*).

Fig. 148.

*Hippolyte varians.*

Our task is now ended—we have endeavoured to give a sketch of the most familiar sea-side objects, and those of the most typical kind, which best illustrate zoological principles. If we have been successful in our compilation, our satisfaction will be complete. One thing will have struck the attentive reader—the abundance of forms of life of which he never dreamt! He has seen they have a life-history which actually exceeds in interest that of the higher animals. And, if he be philosophically disposed, he will feel convinced of the long period of time which has elapsed during which animal life has thus been suited and adapted to every possible physical condition. But none the less will his mind turn with reverence towards the Creatorial Power which has gradually developed this Life-scheme, and rendered it, not a mere freak of Omnipotent force, but a grand plan which unites the most lowly vitalized atom through distinct and oft-times traceable gradations to the Deity Himself!

THE END.

www.ingramcontent.com/pod-product-compliance
Lightning Source LLC
Chambersburg PA
CBHW031956230426
43672CB00010B/2175